Goal-Driven Lesson Planning for Teaching English to Speakers of Other Languages

Marnie Reed
Christina Michaud

Boston University

MICHIGAN TEACHER TRAINING

Ann Arbor
The University of Michigan Press

*To Steven J. Molinsky with appreciation
for the opportunities and the inspiration*

ISBN-13: 978-0-472-03418-5

2013   2012   2011   2010   4   3   2   1

Contents

Introduction

Think about it

Imagine that you're at a job interview for your ideal ESL teaching job. The interview is going well, when the interviewer asks you a key question—"What is your philosophy of teaching?" How do you respond?

The Introduction includes these topics:

- ☑ Using this book
- ☑ Re-imagining what it means to be a language teacher
- ☑ Solving common teaching problems
- ☑ Setting aside distractions to language teaching

Using This Book

If you are reading this book, you are interested in maximizing the effectiveness of your teaching. You've probably looked at at least a few other books on ESL teaching or full of ESL activities: there are many such books out there, some with excellent suggestions for discussion starters, shorter or longer communicative activities, role-plays, etc. This book is not a collection of activities or ready-made lesson plans for you to add to your teaching repertoire. Instead, this book is meant to empower you as a teacher and help you create a principled framework or philosophy for your own teaching—a framework that will shape the varied activities of the ESL classroom into a coherent teaching and learning partnership for you and your students. When you finish reading this book, you should be able to articulate your own individual teaching philosophy.

This book shows you how to use any item of English language materials—an assigned text, a random newspaper article, or an ESL activity from a website—to teach your students *something about language*. The book walks you through the process of reflecting on your role in diagnosing what that "something" is—what your students really need—and planning how you will get them there and how you will know when they got there in a goal-driven, principled manner.

This book is meant to empower you as a teacher. Language motivates, and language empowers. When you set specific language goals and enable students to achieve them, you empower your students and give them the tools for real success in English. When you set aside the many perceived problems and distractions to the task of teaching and focus instead on setting specific language goals and following through on them, you empower yourself as a teacher to bring about real change in your students' language production.

How Is This Book Organized?

Chapter 1 addresses the theory of setting specific language goals for students and offers examples of these in action. Chapter 2 relates this idea of specific language goals to actual learner needs and gives examples of an initial diagnostic and needs-analysis. Chapter 3 redefines lesson planning and offers walk-throughs and templates to use when planning goal-driven language lessons. Chapters 4 and 5 discuss explicit language instruction, grammar lessons, and treatment of error, while Chapter 6 addresses recognizing and assessing student progress. Chapters 7 and 8 tackle the mechanics and logistics that facilitate the goal-driven language classroom, demystifying the transition from a goal-driven lesson plan to the real-time, in-class delivery of the plan.

The Eye-Opener sections highlight surprising facts about language instruction while the Spotlight on Research sections introduce relevant and useful information from TESOL literature.

This book does not separately discuss business English, academic English, conversational English, or English for Specific Purposes. Although these divisions are certainly useful for defining content, specifying sets of vocabulary, and teaching situation-specific pragmatic knowledge, they are beyond the scope and goals of this book. The classroom is primarily a language classroom, and *language-focused goals* for your students should underlie every ESL class, whether it's business English or not.

Some sections refer you to other books or materials. Some teachers find that their curriculum is set, and they cannot introduce additional materials into the classroom; others find that they have no curriculum at all and are in effect responsible for creating their own. In both cases, we believe that effective, efficient teaching can occur: the teaching framework is more than just the materials, which are really secondary to it. However, teachers creating their own curriculum or supplementing one will find useful suggestions here.

 A few sections of this book are flagged with a tutoring icon to address the particulars of working one-on-one (or in very small groups) with students.

Re-Imagining What It Means to Be a Language Teacher

 ### Reflections on Teaching: Creating and Using a Teaching Journal

Regardless of your classroom situation, we encourage you to keep a separate notebook for the journal activities you'll find in this book. Each chapter contains at least one reflective journal item, in which you'll need to think and write thoughtfully about your role as a teacher and the other topics. Each chapter also may contain short question-and-answer activities, designed to prompt further thinking. Stop and think through each activity, exploring possible answers to the journal questions, before continuing to read each chapter.

WHAT ARE YOUR STRENGTHS AS A TEACHER?
WHAT DO YOU DO WELL IN THE CLASSROOM?

    If you don't yet have classroom experience, think about your interactions in business, social activities, and your personal life because many of these strengths transfer into teaching.
    A few examples are:

- thinking on your feet and improvising
- organizing, planning ahead, and making lists
- empathizing with students
- quickly evaluating a problem and resolving it
- setting goals and keeping them clearly in mind
- creating a warm classroom environment
- offering good models of English grammar and pronunciation
- being sensitive to cultural differences
- managing time efficiently and covering material as planned
- choosing interesting topics and materials

 REFLECTIVE JOURNAL

This requires you to think about and actually list your goals.

1. What desires or frustrations prompted you to pick up this book? What goals do you have for yourself as a teacher?

2. What goals do you have for your students? How would you describe your current or prospective English class?

What do you think is important to focus on before a class? Use a check mark to indicate what is most important. Explain why.

1. ____ **interpersonal aspects:** enjoying/creating a bond with students

2. ____ **organizational aspects:** using organized systems for teaching and keeping track of the class (attendance book, handouts organized, etc.)

3. ____ **content aspects:** providing good content (interesting topics for discussion, etc.)

4. ____ **activity level:** relying on a good list of activities

5. ____ **goal level:** establishing clearly set goals for students and knowing how students will reach these goals and how you'll know when they have reached them

Eye-Opener

> While all of these aspects—interpersonal, organizational, content, activity, goal—are important considerations for the classroom, many teachers think of them separately, without giving enough importance to what we think should be the most important aspect—the level of goal-setting.

This book focuses mainly on goal-setting and organization for the classroom; you supply the empathy with your students, the interpersonal aspects, without which you probably wouldn't be teaching or tutoring to begin with. The content of the class can come from you, your students, your textbooks, or your program, but it should not be the driving force in the classroom. Similarly, while it's good to explore a variety of types of activities, and while teachers are always on the lookout for engaging activities that genuinely work in the classroom, the activity should not be an end in itself.

This book provides a framework to take these separate aspects and integrate them into a coherent approach to teaching.

In Figure 1, the items on the left depict how some teachers may approach teaching: everything is separate, compartmentalized, but empathy and activities receive the bulk of the teachers' attention. On the right, an integrated teaching framework is shown, with more attention paid to classroom goals and organization.

FIGURE 1
Two Views of Teaching

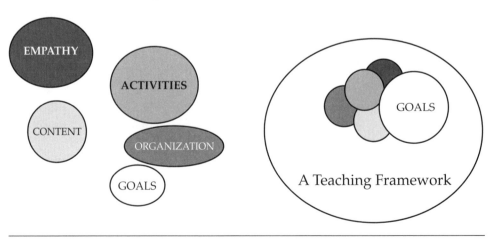

REFLECTIVE JOURNAL

The idea of metacognition is a very important one in educational research and pedagogy. Its benefits have long been recognized in philosophy and psychology, dating back to the ancient Greeks' dictum to "Know thyself." So, here and throughout the book, we challenge you to get to know yourself better as a teacher and to re-examine your experiences, inspirations, and goals through these reflective sections.

Some of the ideas in this introduction may be new to you. At the end of this introduction, flip back through these pages and take specific note of any sections that raised new questions in your mind.

The box on page 4 asked you to consider your strengths as a teacher. This exercise can be a difficult one. It's worthwhile to think about what you do well as a teacher because these strengths are often the reason you turned to teaching in the first place. For example, a teacher who knows he or she relates well to people from other cultures may have turned to teaching ESL (as an avocation or profession) for this reason.

This book will help you address the areas of your teaching that you may feel overwhelmed by at the moment but will also help you build on your known strengths to create an individual teaching style within a principled framework.

The next section is meant to be completed in writing in your journal so that you will be able to look back at your initial responses later. However, use pages 7–9 for your notes; you may also want to talk through these questions with a fellow teacher or a mentor. The two main benefits of this conversation are to create an audience for your thoughts to force yourself to be more specific and articulate in your responses and to create a teaching support network for yourself.

1. Describe your teaching situation if you have one. If you don't have one yet, go to #2.

2. Teachers tend to teach the way they have been taught. Who were some of your best or most memorable teachers, and why do you value them? What do you recall about your experiences learning to read in your first language, learning to speak another language, or living or traveling abroad?

3. Many teachers think that student motivation is an essential component of the classroom and that their job as teachers is to motivate their students. In fact, however, people tend to be motivated most by real outcomes, which vary widely by individual (some learners focus on a high grade in a class, or the possibility of a better job, for instance). Your students' particular motivations are secondary and largely irrelevant to the classroom and to your job. To help realize this, think about a time when you were "motivated" to do something by a focus on goals. Describe the experience.

4. Complete this sentence:

   My job as a teacher is to

Possible responses to this include:

a. *My job is to convey knowledge—for example, teaching the difference between past tense and present perfect.*

   This idea forces teachers into the role of a reference book or library, a position that can paralyze teachers and distract them from their goals if they don't immediately know the answer to a given question. Instead, you as the teacher do not have to be the repository of all knowledge on English.

b. *My job is to be my students' friend. I need to be supportive and make the learning experience enjoyable for students.*

   This view misses the point of having a teacher in the classroom—you should be more of a facilitator than a friend, and the new abilities that students walk away from your classroom with are what make the learning experience truly valuable to them. Furthermore, offering students the language they really need is in fact a measurable way to be their friend and advocate.

c. *My job is to motivate students and make them work harder.*

   This idea misunderstands the role of motivation in the classroom: whatever motivation brought students into your classroom, it's their progress and success that will actually motivate them to return.

d. *My job is to create an environment for students to maximize their potential.*

   This view is just too vague to be useful: if you *do* succeed in reaching this goal, at best all you have is the environment. You don't actually have any measurable achievements or learning.

 Eye-Opener

> Your job as a teacher of ESL is to enable students to reach the
> language goals that you have set.

This formulation of your job as a teacher is useful because it's

1. student-focused
2. language-based (not based on content, atmosphere, or motivation)
3. observable, measurable, and achievable.

Solving Common Teaching Problems

Although there are lots of things to think about before setting foot in the classroom, there are certain things you don't need to worry about. The "problems" listed on pages 11–14 are often part of the realities of teaching; if your overall focus is on yourself as a language teacher and goal-setter for your students, you should be able to work within the framework of any institution.

Problem 1:

Restricted Content/Materials: *The curriculum/book is chosen for me, and I'm locked in to using it.*

It doesn't matter what content you use to teach language. Use any content you have, but set goals for students for language skills. Use the content to help them reach these goals.

CASE STUDY: THE FOOD PYRAMID

A teacher working in a community center was assigned to teach a lesson on the food pyramid and government dietary guidelines to a group of adult learners. The teacher was very unhappy about the required content of this part of his course, and he felt that it was offensive for him to be telling other adults how to eat.

He wasn't focusing, however, on the many language goals that could arise from this required content. Aside from the fact that his learners should be familiar with the content because they will also encounter it in other contexts (doctors' offices, children's schools, etc.), this content lends itself to a grammatical focus on

- numbers
- count/noncount nouns: *milk, rice, bread*
- partitives and plurals: *a glass of milk, a bunch of bananas, a loaf of bread*
- modals: *I should eat more. . .*
- *wh-* questions: *How many vegetables do you eat a day?*

Problem 2:

Specialization: *I'm supposed to teach business English (or another specialized field), and I don't have extensive experience in that field.*

It doesn't matter—you're teaching language. The content is set, so just fill in some vocabulary items. If students are already taking business or technological English, they may be good informants about what kinds of vocabulary they need to know. You as teachers can predict the language students will ultimately need in this context; work backward from your mental script of what students will need to say.

Problem 3:

Open-Ended Content/Materials: *There is no set curriculum. How am I going to find materials to fill every session?*

Find something you like and your students don't hate—newspapers, current events, holidays/cultural items—and use these things as the content of your class. Remember that you're teaching language *through* the content; you're not teaching content.

Problem 4:

Administrative Pressures: *My school/department is very rigid in its guidelines for teachers. I've been asked to speak more slowly or simply.*

Many language programs are run with very specific and inflexible guidelines for teachers. For example, if the main focus of a program is to get students to stay in class and re-enroll for another semester, then allowing students to reply only in a few words or with very inaccurate grammar may be tolerated. While you probably can't change the system at an entire institution, you often *can* work within the system to use meaningful language, set specific language goals for students, and achieve higher levels of student accuracy within your classroom. In every case, be sure you understand the political climate of your institution.

Problem 5:

Class Size: *My classes are too big. I have 20–30 students in a room. OR I'm nervous about being one-on-one with a student as a tutor*

In general, teachers and tutors have no control over the number of students in their class. If you're lucky enough to have the ideal class size (8–15 or so), that's great. If not, this is one of the realities that you have to accept.

Problem 6:

Affective Factors: *I don't want to make students feel bad about their accent or their mistakes.*

Remember that your job as teacher or tutor is not to be the students' friend. It's possible to set up a classroom climate that doesn't stigmatize students' accents or mistakes, and that also doesn't tolerate inaccuracy on targeted grammar/pronunciation points. Students come to class wanting—and often needing—to improve, which usually means changing their accents or grammar. As teachers, we are not serving students well if we don't call attention to inaccuracies and provide the means for them to change their language patterns to reach the language goals.

Problem 7:

Multiple Levels of Students in One Class: *I'm worried that students will be at multiple levels in my classroom. How can I keep the advanced students entertained?*

Varying levels within one classroom is a fact of life, and not one that you should spend a great time of time worrying about. In general, identify the error patterns your students have in common—almost all learners will share problems with noun and verb endings, for example, or with word- and sentence-level stress. In addition, you can often use the different ability levels in your classroom to your advantage. Sometimes you may want to group students by ability levels for a specific activity, and sometimes you may want to pair a more advanced student with a less-proficient one.

Problem 8:

Unstable Enrollment: *My class enrollment is always changing, with some new students coming in every few weeks. I'm worried about continuity.*

Don't worry about this! New students mean opportunities to recycle old classroom expectations and recycle your teaching points. Use your continuing students as informants for the new ones: students genuinely like being able to show off what they've learned, and you'll be able to assess exactly where your continuing students are. You can even use this strategy if your enrollment doesn't change over the course of the semester, but your students have spotty attendance.

Problem 9:

Feeling Overwhelmed: *My students have so many needs. How will I ever be able to help them make the progress they need? OR I don't know anything about my students' native language(s), and I'm worried I won't be able to help them as well as I could if I did.*

Remember that your job as a teacher is to set specific language goals and give learners what they need to achieve them. You don't need to know everything about English or about your students' language(s) in order to do this. Calm down, figure out what your students need (i.e., what errors are they making?), and prioritize a set of goals for them.

In addition, resources like *Learner English* can help you anticipate errors, as will experience, but you should get your students focused on analyzing the difference between their native languages and English. You don't need to have all the answers; this process of analysis actually helps the students.

Problem 10:

Motivation: *What if my students aren't motivated to work hard at their language? What if different students in the class have different motivations?*

Teachers tend to think that student motivation is the first and necessary step toward language success. However, our goal-driven approach to teaching can lead your students directly toward language success—which in turn may result in increasing students' motivation. Furthermore, we can find out students' stated reasons for attending a class, but we never really know what's going on in their heads, and even if we did, students' stated motivation is largely irrelevant to what goes on in the classroom. You can't control who ended up in your room or for what reason, but you *can* control what you do in the classroom. If you set specific language goals and enable students to reach those goals, students will become motivated. It's students' own choice whether or not to use the new pattern they've learned in their everyday speech or writing, but if they are able to do it (i.e., they've reached the goal), you have done your job. Tell students explicitly why they're doing specific things; focus students on the payoff. Your goal should not be to "get students motivated" or even to have them motivate themselves; if you have specific language goals for your students, that's all you need to focus on.

These "problems" are not obstacles to classroom success. They are, however, distractions from the real work of teaching and learning language. As teachers, we need to set aside these concerns and focus on the real work of the classroom—goal-driven lesson planning and delivery.

Setting Aside Distractions to Language Teaching

Some teachers distract themselves from the real work of the classroom by allowing and elaborating on all possible tangents in a discussion or by resisting giving closure through simple, discussion-ending answers.

Based on our years of training and supervising pre-service and in-service teachers, we present this list of things teachers hate to say:

1. *That's beyond the scope of our lesson.* Don't be afraid to say this to students. If you've got specific language goals and steps to get students to those goals, you'll know instantly whether something is or is not outside the scope of the lesson, and you will not need to debate with yourself in the classroom about whether or not a particular tangent is or is not relevant. Once you've decided that a particular question is irrelevant, you will need to shut down discussion on it firmly and re-direct students back to the goal at hand.

2. *That's just the way it is (in English / in this case).* There are times when this is in fact the right answer to a student's question. Teachers are often comfortable giving this response about something fairly simple, such as irregular forms of nouns or verbs. However, with more advanced and non-systematic grammar points (such as which verbs take gerunds vs. infinitives, which verbs take which prepositions, and which verbs are transitive vs. intransitive), teachers often unnecessarily second-guess themselves and are reluctant to simply state the reality that some aspects of language are not predictable. On the other hand, students often welcome this kind of straightforward response.

3. *You'll have to memorize it.* Since some aspects of language are not predictable or rule-governed, there are words, forms, and patterns that students simply must memorize, just as native speakers do (whether or not they recall doing so). Teachers are often reluctant to say this because it makes them feel that they are inadequate to explaining the task at hand or may bring to mind associations with out-of-vogue teaching styles (such as pattern-practice drills). Students, on the other hand, are used to memorization: academic-level ESL students typically memorize dates, facts, formulas, etc., in their other subjects, while community or literary-level ESL learners will have already had to memorize the basic elements of literacy and language. In fact, most teachers will remember that they had to memorize to do well in school themselves.

4. *No, that's wrong.* This may be one of the most difficult things for teachers to bring themselves to say, but it is sometimes necessary and helpful. (Chapter 2 discusses how and under what circumstances to respond to student errors in the classroom.) Beyond direct language errors, however, this situation sometimes arises when students have firm but mistaken convictions. For example, one student we know was insistent that contractions, which characterize American English, are "lazy" English and are not used by speakers of British English. The reality is, of course, that both British and American speakers do contract; it would not serve anyone for a teacher to argue back and forth with an insistent student on this point, nor would it be helpful to allow the misperception to persist in the classroom. Teachers need to feel comfortable, in such situations, saying, "No, that's not the case," and re-directing the class as a whole back to the goals at hand. (As a side note, you may want to ask an individual student—as the teacher in this case did—to check his or her facts and discuss it with you later, but the point is to control the discourse of the classroom in a clear, goal-focused way because you know where students need to be.)

REFLECTIVE JOURNAL

Do you have an overall approach to teaching? Can you articulate it? Would an observer in your classroom on any random day see things that match that approach?

What do you hope to gain from this book? How do you think it might affect your approach to teaching?

Setting Specific Language Goals

If you walk into a random ESL classroom on a random day, the teacher in that class will tell you the topic of the lesson: Past participles, Family vocabulary, or *wh-* questions and answers. If that teacher were asked *why* he or she was teaching that topic, however, there might be resistance. If pressed, a teacher might then answer that *why* question by saying something like:

"We already did _____, so now we're up to this."
"This was next on the syllabus."
"We're supposed to cover this at this level."

What's the problem with these responses? How might a more goal-focused teacher respond to the same question?

Chapter 1 includes these topics:

☑ Using specific language goals as the motivation for any given lesson

☑ Setting specific language goals: Rationale and examples

☑ Reverse-engineering teachers' goals from students' performance

☑ Setting goals according to students' true language needs

☑ Overcoming distractions that divert attention from setting goals

Using Specific Language Goals as the Motivation for Any Given Lesson

As this example demonstrates, teachers may sometimes be unable to state their reasons for teaching specific topics at given times other than in terms of course requirements. A goal-focused teacher would respond to the *why* question by referring to students' progress in meeting ongoing language goals: "They need past participles because next week we're going to work on the passive voice." Or, "My students need to be able to answer the questions on the citizenship exam." Having specific language goals for your students, therefore, means that you as a teacher will always be able to answer the *why* question. If *you* know why you're teaching something, it's possible to make it transparent to your students.

Setting Specific Language Goals: Rationale and Examples

A goal-focused approach includes specific language goals stated from the students' perspective. Goals (or objectives) are not the same as a lesson topic.

Teacher-Described Lesson Topics	Student-Focused Goals (Objectives):
"I'm going to cover past participles today, regular and irregular."	Students will be able to form the past participles for target irregular verbs, form the past participles for regular verbs, and pronounce them correctly.

These student-focused goals should be observable and measurable, *operationalized*.

Writing Operationalized Objectives

How do you know when your objectives are concrete and operationalized? Consider this sample objective:

> Students will explore the main ideas of the three articles and share their views.

Less effective goal statements talk around the final outcome, rather than define it; therefore, no one knows when this objective has been achieved. Avoid these words to help keep the objective concrete.

explore	understand	learn more about
know	realize	improve
review	practice	share

Consider this rewritten objective:

> Students will state the main idea of each article using the attributive verbs *say*, *think*, *state*, *assert*, and *claim* accurately and appropriately.

More effective objectives use concrete words, specific examples, and non-ambiguous language. These objectives present the measures to know when they have been reached. These objectives clearly define the final outcome. It's possible to set this kind of operationalized language goal at levels from beginning to advanced. For students at a beginning level, for example, you may have a goal as simple—but still measurable and observable—as this:

> Students will respond appropriately to the question "What's your name?"

As students' language skills advance, the content of your goals should advance along with them, but the form of the goals will generally vary quite little.

Reverse-Engineering Teachers' Goals from Students' Performance

To test out the claim that operationalized, observable objectives are helpful in the classroom, it should be possible to arrive at a teacher's objectives by observing student outcomes. In other words, what do you see happening in the classroom? What are students doing or saying? Working backward from what you observe, you should be able to articulate the result of the lesson. Whether or not a teacher had these specific objectives in mind, consciously or unconsciously, before teaching the lesson, this is what students are actually able to do and say as a result of the lesson.

Find an ESL class to observe. This should be fairly easy; most programs are happy to accommodate, with advance notice, a new teacher in the spirit of mentoring and professional development. When you observe the lesson, what do you think you should focus your attention on?

If you focus on these things in the classroom—types of activities, grouping, or participation from different students—you will be analyzing the lesson on a surface level. There is of course value in considering the teacher's decisions with regard to grouping, the different types of activities that occurred during the lesson, and the range of participation from both shy and vocal students, but your analysis of the lesson cannot stop at this point.

You will also need to think more specifically about the students' participation: what are the students saying? Describe the language they are using. Your notes during the lesson should include enough of the language that students are using so that you can reconstruct both what they were talking about and how accurate they were in their use of the language.

Imagine that you're observing a class with students who have just read for homework a passage on soil erosion in the Southwest. The teacher asks students what they recall from the reading, and students volunteer various details from the text, starting with their complaints about how long the reading took them to do. As you listen to the discussion, you of course hear grammatical errors, which you are interested in transcribing to look at more closely later. However, you don't have to write every word that every student says to capture their errors. The chart shows what individual students actually said in the classroom, what they probably meant (given the context), and what you may have written in order to remind you of the error for later analysis.

The student said. . .	The student probably meant. . .	You transcribed the error as. . .
I took three hour to read.	It took me three hours. . .	I took three hour. . .
All the new word were difficult.	All the new words. . .	All the new word. . .
It's make it very difficult.	It makes. . .	It's make. . .
Soil use-ed for growing food.	. . . used. . .	Soil use-ed for growing. . .
Is evenly distribute. . .	It's evenly distributed. . .	Is evenly distribute. . .
The nation with surplus food. . .	(All) the nations with. . .	(All) the nation with surplus. . .

Then think back to the lesson, and look at your notes to answer the questions on the checklist.

Checklist for observing a lesson:

- Ask yourself these key questions while observing any classroom lesson:
  - ☐ What was the teacher's objective for the lesson? How do you know?
- Remember to state the objective(s) in operationalized terms from the students' perspective—what are students able to do/say now, at the end of the lesson, that they weren't before?
  - ☐ Look closely at the language that the students used during the lesson. Your notes will be very helpful here.
  - ☐ Are there repeated structures that caused students to make mistakes, perhaps initially, but that they then received instruction and/or correction in?
  - ☐ Are there differences between the kind of language (and the level of accuracy) that students were producing at the beginning and end of the lesson?
  - ☐ What can you tell about the language that the teacher is using? What is the "teaching talk," the succinct, minimal language of instruction?
  - ☐ How does that teaching talk (if you observed it) relate to the language students are producing at the end of the lesson?

ACTIVITY: A SAMPLE CLASSROOM OBSERVATION

Imagine that you observed a lesson in which students have just finished reading the first section of an English language novel. This is their first discussion of the novel in the classroom. Most of the students report that they found the reading difficult. To analyze the source of the problem, the teacher asks students to share with their classmates passages in the reading that they individually found difficult. You take these notes, among others, of students' speech during the first part of the lesson:

S1: In the page thirty-three. . . On the chapter three . . .

S2: On page-ee seven. . .

S3: On page one-four-seven. . .

S4: On one paragraph. . . (the first paragraph)

You also notice when the teacher corrects students and addresses language patterns explicitly:

> *T*: We use *on* for pages and *in* for paragraphs and chapters. Don't say *the* if you use a number.
>
> *T*: Page. One syllable.
>
> *T*: Read it as a single number.
>
> *T*: We use *in* for paragraphs, and tell us specifically where on the page. *In the first paragraph. . .*

You observe that students notice when they are being corrected, and toward the end of the lesson you hear this:

> *S1*: In page—on page 27. . .
>
> *S2*: On page ten. . .
>
> *S3*: On page one hundred and four. . .
>
> *S4*: On one paragraph. . .   *T*: In which paragraph?   *S4*: In the first paragraph. . .

An observer may note that there was some pair work and then a full-class discussion and may even think that the teacher's only goal was "getting students to talk about the text." This lesson goes beyond that, however, and the teacher had specific objectives for students. What do you think? How would you state the teacher's objectives based on the notes and data you have?

Maybe you think the objective is that students will be able to find a specific spot on a page. This is close, but you can be more specific. What are students saying and doing at the end of the lesson, as opposed to at the beginning?

Students are. . .

- identifying a passage by page and paragraph number.
- able to use correct prepositions for pages, paragraphs, and chapters.
- able to say the word *page* as a one-syllable word.
- able to use cardinal and ordinal numbers appropriately in this context.

What you have just done, by observing a lesson and paying close attention to the language students and teachers are using, is to re-create the specific, observable objectives that a good teacher may have had in mind when planning the lesson. You should always look for objectives when observing a lesson; conversely, a visitor to your classroom should be able to state your objectives by observing what your students do and say.

Setting Specific Goals for Favorite Activities

Most teachers have a favorite go-to activity that always works to get students talking and engaged, but teachers might not have taken this activity to the next level and analyzed the language and related language goals it involves. Setting specific language goals for your students can help you maximize the effectiveness of any activity (reading, topic, etc.) that you would do in the classroom.

Look at the chart on pages 24–25, and then think of some activities of your own and how you might extend them in this manner.

Step 1: Think of an activity you typically use in the classroom.

Step 2: Brainstorm the different language topics (grammar, vocabulary, pronunciation) involved in the implementation of that activity.

Step 3: Script what students will actually be saying (the language product of the task) when they successfully complete the activity.

Step 4: On the basis of your brainstorms and your scripts, draft student-focused, observable, measurable language goals for the activity.

Setting Goals According to Students' True Language Needs

At the first meeting between a tutor and an ESL learner, after exchanging names and pleasantries, this conversation took place. The learner was visibly pregnant.

T: How far along are you?

S: Not far—I live in Watertown.

T: Oh. . . uh, right, that's not far. I live in Cambridge.

What's the problem with this exchange? Regardless of what the learner articulates about her goals and interests for this and future tutoring sessions, what does this exchange tell you about the learner's real-world language needs?

An informal survey we conducted reveals that many teachers are on the side of the tutor in this example: many teachers agree that they, too, would have responded to the student's off-target answer and pursued that line of conversation. When pressed, one teacher explained that she wouldn't have wanted to embarrass the student by pointing out her misunderstanding. All of these teachers have missed the point, however: the pregnant ESL learner is going to be asked this (admittedly idiomatic) question at numerous points in the next few

From Activity to Goals

Topic/Reading/ Activity	Language of the Task	Language Goals for Students
What would you do if you won the lottery? (imaginative discussion)	• conditional *would* • contracted *would* (*I'd,* etc.) • word-initial /w/ (vs. *oud*) and lack of consonant /l/ (vs. *wooled*) • *wh-* questions • contrastive stress<hr>I'd donate some of the money and travel around the world. What would *you* do?	Students will be able to: • ask and answer questions with *would* appropriately • pronounce *would* correctly • pronounce contracted *would* correctly • ask for help with new vocabulary they want to use in their responses (*How do you say. . . . ?*) • increase pitch, volume, and duration of contrastively stressed pronoun where appropriate
Should students be allowed to look at their cell phones during class? (class debate)	• yes/no questions with *should* lack of consonant /l/ (vs. *shooled*) • short answers with yes/no and *should* • complex sentences with *because* • agree/disagree + *with* + person • impersonal *you* modals (*might, could,* etc.) • discourse markers for contrast (*but, on the other hand*)<hr>Yes, because you might need to call home. I agree with John. There could be an emergency.	Students will be able to: • ask and answer yes/no questions with *should* • pronounce *should* correctly • form complex sentences with *because* in their answers • use the impersonal *you* to state generalities • use modal *might* and *could* appropriately in their answers • use *agree* appropriately as an intransitive verb • use constrastive discourse markers appropriately to separate ideas

Topic/Reading/ Activity	Language of the Task	Language Goals for Students

months, both by new acquaintances and by doctors, nurses, and reception-ists at medical appointments. She *needs* to be able to respond appropriately to this question; furthermore, she likely has additional language needs with vocabulary and other idioms related to her pregnancy.

In this situation, preserving a superficial level of communication and ignoring the basic misunderstanding does not serve the student. We as teach-ers (and tutors) may find ourselves in situations like this, where we recog-nize a language need our students may not themselves see. Our task then is to see and take advantage of opportunities for setting specific language goals for our students.

Overcoming Distractions that Divert Attention from Setting Goals

Teaching Frustrations

One thing that distracts teachers is their own frustrations with their job. The chart on page 27 lists some of these job-related frustrations and very briefly introduces the solutions to these problems that will be developed more throughout this book.

REFLECTIVE JOURNAL

Often, current or future ESL/EFL teachers say they want to be more comfort-able and confident in the classroom. The idea of achieving confidence in your teaching as a goal in and of itself, however, is a flawed one. Other teachers merely say that they want to "become better teachers," which is so broad a goal as to be meaningless. This book will refocus your attention away from yourself and your teaching and onto your students and their learning. By focusing on learners, setting achievable language goals for them, and mea-suring their progress toward those goals, you will discover that you have, in fact, "become a better teacher," which will provide a genuine basis for confi-dence in your teaching. What do you think?

How easy is it for you to focus on learners, as opposed to focusing on your-self as a teacher?

What are your opinions on the student-focused goals—as opposed to the teacher-described lesson topics—and their importance?

Where would you stand in the tutor-learner exchange detailed on pages 23 and 26?

Teacher's Frustration

Class preparation takes too much time.	This book directly addresses this issue. The key is envisioning where students need to be, then working backward from there. At that point, the lessons will almost plan themselves.
Students don't like the topics of some of the readings.	That's okay! Students need to know *why* they're doing a specific activity—they're not here to learn about a specific topic, since activities are just in service of larger language goals. Effective lesson-planning helps address this issue and makes transparent to the students the reason why they are doing something. In other words, it doesn't matter if they don't like the content of a given reading/activity: students can see they are learning something about English, with the content as a vehicle.
Students do the activities, but they don't seem to make real progress.	Unfortunately, this is the inevitable outcome if students are only asked to fill out exercises on their own; instead, teachers have to make transparent for students the connection from individual exercises/activities to their own use of the language.
Grading is stressful and takes too much time.	Grading doesn't have to be time-consuming, or subjective. If you grade with a specific list of criteria in mind, even long compositions filled with errors are not difficult to get through.
My students are all at different levels—I just want an activity everyone can do.	Even the perfect activity isn't a solution to every classroom problem. Teachers need to consider the common needs among the different students in their class and focus the activity on students' genuine needs.
I can't focus on accuracy and meaning at the same time.	You can. If your goals for students are completely clear to you, and if you know exactly which language features you are monitoring for accuracy, then this becomes a manageable task. (See Chapter 5 for more information on this issue.)

Analyzing Student Needs

Imagine that you are teaching your first course at a language school. You've talked with the program director ahead of time and inherited a syllabus and textbook from former teachers of this level. On your first day in the classroom, however, you are suddenly overwhelmed by the number and variety of mistakes that students are making. What do you do now? How do you sort through these mistakes to decide what to address?

Chapter 2 includes these topics:

- ☑ Facing the problem of learner errors
- ☑ Implementing a solution—Diagnosing learner errors
- ☑ Using a theoretical framework to model learner progress
- ☑ Creating needs analysis plans for one-on-one tutoring, small group tutorials, and more formal classes

Facing the Problem of Learner Errors

Chapter 1 addressed the issue of setting goals for students based on their language needs (not interests or student-perceived needs). But how do you determine those needs? Even a teacher who's committed to a goal-driven approach to language may encounter one of these problems when attempting to diagnose student needs:

- **not noticing student errors**. Sometimes, especially when teaching an advanced group of students, teachers may have a false sense of learners' abilities. Particularly if students are outgoing or willing to speak up, teachers may not really notice students' inaccuracies, paying attention instead to the amount of language students are producing and the content. In this case, we suggest using formal diagnostics (detailed on pages 37–46), ideally in conjunction with a recorder, to accurately gauge learners' levels.

- **feeling overwhelmed by student errors.** As in the situation described, some teachers quickly become aware that students have language needs, but they may feel overwhelmed by the complexity of the problem. What they are facing is on one level a problem of data complexity: the need is to sort through and make sense of student errors, deciding which are more serious and which are within the scope of the level or timeframe.

- **accommodating one's ear to student errors.** Some teachers accommodate their ears to students' errors; Varonis and Gass (1982) examined causes of communication breakdown and found that "language teachers, due to their familiarity with nonnative accents, must guard against becoming tolerant, since the goal is to prepare ESL students to be understood by those less linguistically trained (i.e., less tolerant) outside the classroom."

Addressing the Problem: What's Holding Us Back?

ESL teachers play multiple roles in interacting with their students: they may be formal or informal advisors and cultural informants, offering information on negotiating life in the United States, but primarily they are language instructors. This constant juggling of roles sometimes gives teachers an identity crisis as they try to determine their role in the classroom. The chart on page 31 shows some of the differences between these different roles.

Conversational Partners	Language Instructors
let students' desires and interests guide conversation	let student needs and language goals guide conversation
lean in empathetically when students are soft-spoken	lean back and encourage students to speak to the class
gloss over student errors	focus on target student errors to help them self-correct and build independence
focus on fluency and content	focus on accuracy and content

SPOTLIGHT ON RESEARCH

How can I focus on form—i.e., students' accuracy—without harming students' sense of identity?

Ellis, Basturkmen, and Loewen (2001) reported on learner uptake in "focus-on-form" episodes in 12 hours of communicative language teaching. Not only did students not shut down when corrected, but uptake was more likely when learner errors were addressed explicitly rather than implicitly.

Implementing a Solution— Diagnosing Learner Errors

Whatever group of students you have, some problems will be common to learners, even those from a variety of language backgrounds, and will include errors with noun and verb endings, articles, stress patterns, spelling, and pronunciation of sounds (such as the *th* sound in *think* and *the*) that are rare in the world's languages.

Of these, article errors—though pervasive—are generally considered to be less serious and less teachable than, for example, errors with noun and verb endings. Errors with these endings are highly stigmatizing to students and seriously impair their communication with other speakers. But noun and verb endings are systematic and rule-governed, so learners can be taught to produce them accurately.

Other errors are specific to learners' particular first-language backgrounds. A useful reference book for these errors is *Learner English* (Cambridge University Press, Swann and Smith, 2nd ed., 2001), which has chapters detailing the problems specific to 22 different languages or language groups. This book is particularly helpful if you're teaching EFL/ESL in a monolingual environment. If you're teaching a more heterogeneous group of learners, however, a quick look at the different chapters representing your students' first languages will show you the common areas of difficulty in your class.

Beyond these predictable errors, however, you will likely be faced with a myriad of grammar, pronunciation, and vocabulary errors even on the first day of class. Some teachers may be tempted to just ask students what their biggest mistakes are, in order to address these errors more quickly. This approach does not generally work.

SPOTLIGHT ON RESEARCH

According to Derwing and Rossiter (2002):

"When we asked respondents what pronunciation problems they typically experienced, 39 out of 100 participants were unable to identify specific areas of difficulty.

Eighty-four percent of the specific problems identified by the remaining 61 students were segmentals [such as] 'th' [and] 'l/r.'

If a speaker makes mistakes with the suprasegmentals, listeners will sometimes not have enough information to understand the message—even if all the individual sounds (the segmentals) were correct."

Even beyond the field of pronunciation, ESL learners are not cognizant of their language errors. If, at the beginning of a grammar-based course, you ask students what their biggest mistakes are, you are likely to hear answers such as "verbs" or "vocabulary," which are so broad as to be unhelpful.

Using a Theoretical Framework
to Model Learner Progress

As a result, we say that learners at the beginning of a course typically don't know what they don't know.

A MODEL OF LEARNER PROGRESS:
HOW STUDENTS BECOME UNCONSCIOUSLY COMPETENT

Teachers tell students directly that there is bad news and there is good news about their language errors: on one hand, everyone probably has more problems than they are aware of but, on the other hand, no one person makes all possible errors.

Learner progress can be conceptualized as shown in Figure 2 and the chart on page 34.

FIGURE 2 ───────────────────────────────
The Four Levels of Competence

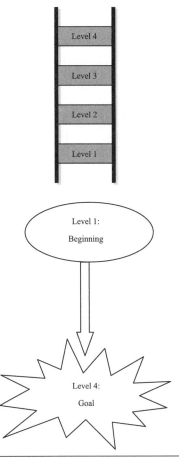

	The Four Levels of Competence	
	Consciousness	Competence
Level 4 Unconscious Competence	-	+
Level 3 Conscious Competence	+	+
Level 2 Conscious Incompetence	+	-
Level 1 Unconscious Incompetence	-	-

Source: *Sound Concepts* by M. Reed and C. Michaud, 2005, McGraw-Hill. Used with permission.

Consciousness means being aware of errors and thinking about how to correct them. *Competence* means not making errors.

You may want to share these levels and the ladder with students at the beginning of a course and periodically throughout to remind students of their progress.

The Four Levels of Competence

At the beginning of instruction in any aspect of language, students are at Level 1 (Unconscious Incompetence). Students make errors, but they are not aware of what their errors are; it is at this stage that teachers gather baseline data (in the form of initial diagnostics, as will be shown later in this chapter).

After some instruction, students gain a conceptual grasp of target sound, pattern, or concept and are at Level 2 (Conscious Incompetence). [How to get students to this level through teaching talk (the language of instruction) and how to tell they're at this level based on student tell-backs—what students are able to tell you back about the rule or strategy you have just introduced—is provided on page 64.]

After instruction and practice, students master specifics of production under teacher control and are at Level 3 (Conscious Competence). [How to get students to this level through a teacher-student partnership (strategic instruction, guided practice, and a principled approach to corrective feedback) and how to tell they're at this level based on teacher-prompted production is provided on page 35.]

After practice, students (start to) form new mental images for the target, at Level 3 or Level 4 (Unconscious Competence). [How to get students to this level through a closed-circuit theory of convergent production and how to tell they're at this level based on student self-correction (Level 3) and student spontaneous production (Level 4) is discussed in Chapter 7.]

It may help to think of the process in another way, as shown in Figure 3.

FIGURE 3————————————————————————————
Teaching Talk and the Role of Prompted Production

Teaching Talk

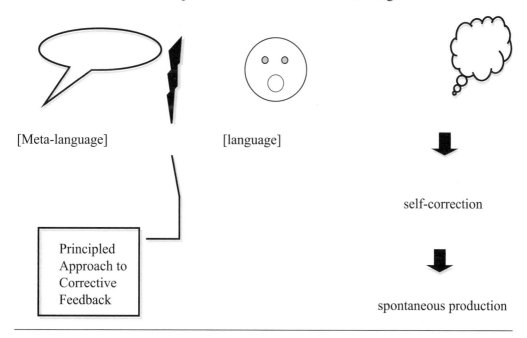

Tell-Backs + Prompted Production ⇒ New Mental Image

[Meta-language]   [language]

                                                    self-correction

Principled
Approach to
Corrective
Feedback   spontaneous production

Creating Needs Analysis Plans
for One-on-One Tutoring, Small Group
Tutorials, and More Formal Classes

1. One-on-One Tutoring

The demand for one-on-one tutors to work with English language learners, usually through programs such as citizenship organizations, faith-based organizations, literacy programs, and libraries, has increased. Such programs typically provide minimal amounts of training for their volunteer tutors. Tutors working one-on-one with learners have a wonderful opportunity to focus solely on a single learner's needs and problems; however, the danger of slipping into the role of merely a conversational partner is particularly great in these cases. Even one-on-one tutors can and should be operating with a goal-driven approach to language teaching—not mere conversing. A first-session diagnostic plan that tutors can implement is detailed.

GUIDELINES FOR THE DIAGNOSTIC INTERVENTION PLAN

Step 1: The Speaking Diagnostic (record and take detailed notes on errors)

The Speaking Diagnostic focuses on pronunciation. It is designed to include all 24 consonant and 15 vowel sounds of English, as well as consonant clusters. It is designed to detect a number of predictable interference problems for speakers of a variety of languages. It is double-spaced to allow teachers to mark the passage to indicate student errors.

> **Preparation**: Prior to meeting with your student, prepare two copies of the Speaking Diagnostic—one for the student to read from and the other for you to mark. If possible, arrange to bring a tape recorder to your first meeting.
>
> **At your first meeting**: ask the student to read the Speaking Diagnostic silently. Then, ideally with recorder running, ask your student to read the Speaking Diagnostic aloud. While the student is reading, mark your copy of the text to indicate errors. Use the recording to refine your error-detection.

DIAGNOSTIC ———————————————————————

> **Directions:** Read the passage silently. When you are
> ready, read the passage aloud.

Most travelers, immigrants, and international students know that they could experience culture shock when they visit a new place. At first, there is what's known as the "honeymoon" phase. At this stage, they're interested in all the new and different things in their new world. Everyone is full of hope, and nothing is too huge a challenge. After that, even though they are prepared, many people are surprised to experience a period of frustration and anxieties. In addition to culture shock, they also experience *language* shock: they question their ability to speak the language, to learn so much new vocabulary, and to pronounce the words. The differences between the new culture and their home that seemed charming at first now seem very insurmountable. For most people, after a period of several months, this stage gives way to one of adjustment, and they are finally able to enjoy the new culture that they had previously experienced as alien. What comes as a major shock to some students and visitors, though, is that after living in their new environment for awhile, it's possible they would find it hard to go back to their home country. They may actually experience *another* kind of culture shock (sometimes called re-entry culture shock) when returning to their home towns and villages.

Intake Interview Assessment

Directions: Use hatch marks to tally errors.

PRONUNCIATION ERRORS

ELEMENT	Number Tally	Examples
Wrong Vowel		
Wrong Consonant		
Final Consonant Deleted		
Consonant Cluster Deletion		
Wrong Number of Syllables: Extra Syllable		
Wrong Number of Syllables: Missing Syllable		
Wrong Syllable Is Stressed		
Missing Contrastive Stress		

MORPHOLOGY ERROR

ELEMENT	Number Tally	Examples
Plural Ending Missing		
Plural Ending Mispronounced		
Past Tense Regular Verb Ending Missing		
Past Tense Regular Ending Mispronounced		
3rd Person Singular Present Tense Ending Missing		
3rd Person Sing. Present Tense Ending Mispronounced		
Past Participle Regular Verb Ending Missing		
Past Participle Regular Verb Ending Mispronounced		
Possessive –'s Ending Missing		
Possessive –'s Ending Mispronounced		
Irregular Plural Ending Missing		
Irregular Plural Ending Mispronounced		
Irregular Past Tense/Participle Ending Missing		
Irregular Past Tense/ Participle Ending Mispronounced		

GRAMMAR ERROR

ELEMENT	Number Tally	Examples
No Subject		
Double Subject		
Count/ Noncount Noun Error		
Noun/ Pronoun Agreement Error		
No Verb		
Verb Tense Error (Missing or Wrong Tense)		
Verb Phrase Error (collocation/ phrasal verb error)		
Wrong Word Form (Part of Speech)		
Subject-Verb Agreement Error		
Topic/ Comment Sentence Structure		
Transitive/ Intransitive Verb Error		
Article Error		
Usage Error (e.g.: *It makes people to think that . . .*)		

The diagnostic on page 37 incorporates known pronunciation problems for the following languages: Arabic, Chinese (Mandarin and Cantonese), Croatian, Dutch, Farsi, Finnish, French, German, Greek, Hungarian, Italian, Japanese, Korean, Portuguese, Russian, Spanish, Swedish, Thai, Turkish, Urdu, and Vietnamese.

Step 2: The Oral Interview (record and take detailed notes on errors)

For the duration of the first meeting, elicit from your student such information as:

- native language/ country of origin
- length of residence in the United States
- length of study of English
- personal/ professional purpose/ goals for the tutoring sessions.

Finally, ask your student to list the specific problems he or she hopes to address in the tutoring session. In other words, you are asking your student to identify his or her problems with English. Remember that students are often not very good at doing this, however.

Step 3: The Diagnostic Intervention Plan

1. List and categorize the errors:
   a. Compare your notes of student errors with the student's self-identified problem areas. Keep in mind that learners rarely have the ability to accurately identify their areas of difficulty or their errors.
   b. Compare your notes of student errors with *Learner English*. Sort by pronunciation, grammar, etc., and by "learnability" considerations.
2. Triage:
   Decide which of the error types you believe you can effectively address in the number of sessions you have before you and target those when writing your goal-driven lesson plans.

2. Small Group Tutorials or Informal Classes

Small group tutorials—some of which work on a drop-in basis—or informal, often community-based classes occupy a middle ground between one-on-one tutoring sessions and more formal classes. Using the information given, draw on tips from the other two sections (see pages 36 and 41) here as they are useful to you.

In small group, drop-in tutorial sessions (often run out of civic centers, libraries, and faith-based organizations) a tutor or teacher may not know how many students will show up—or who they are—until they walk through the door on a given day. In such situations, there are no textbooks or syllabi. Nevertheless, with a goal-driven approach and a language focus (rather than a conversational/content-based focus), teachers can make such drop-in groups actual places for real language change to occur for students.

For example, if you have a two-hour session, in the first few minutes you can do a compressed version of an informal diagnostic. Just by listening to students introduce themselves to others, you can quickly assess general ability levels and glaring needs. You might decide to focus on only two or three basic points that most students have in common, based on your predictions of student errors and your initial mini-diagnostic, such as third-person singular, present tense verb endings (*My roommate always study late at night and it bother me.*), subject-auxiliary inversion in questions (*How old your son?*), and [th] sounds (*Sank you!*). At this point, your job as a tutor/teacher in such a group is to multi-task, controlling the conversation so that the topic moves well and everyone can participate, but also offering explicit instruction in and continued monitoring for your target points.

3. More Formal Classes

In most formal class contexts, you will want to use some sort of formal diagnostic at the beginning of the semester (in addition of course to informal observation and assessment).

Benefits of formal diagnostics:

■ You become quickly aware of student needs and have the ability to set language-based goals accordingly.

■ You collect baseline data of where students are at the beginning of your course to compare to their achievement at the end of your course.

■ You can make transparent to students their actual progress in your course, showing them what specific mistakes they make at the beginning and how that compares to what they do later.

■ You satisfy any administrative requirements of your school or program.

Three kinds of diagnostics are suggested:

1. A basic performative diagnostic, which assesses students' main pronunciation errors (including errors with verb and noun endings).

2. A basic tallysheet for making sense of an initial piece of writing that can be used in any writing your students produce (e.g., brief introductions/biographies, statements about their backgrounds or interests) at the beginning of the course as a baseline diagnostic.

3. A metacognitive diagnostic that can be used in any listening, speaking, or integrated skills class. You do not need to use this entire diagnostic; it does not need to be used all at once; and it does not necessarily need be filled out by students (depending on their levels). It's useful, however, to find out both what students' errors are and how aware students are (recall the levels of competence) of what they do and do not know about English. You may find, if you administer this metacognitive diagnostic both at the beginning and end of a course—and target some of the concepts on it in a goal-driven way in the middle—that students make a small amount of progress correcting their own errors but a lot of progress identifying and understanding the source of their errors. That, in and of itself, is progress, as students move from Level 1 to Levels 2 or 3 on the ladder.

SPEAKING DIAGNOSTIC ─────────────────────────────

How is your speaking? Let's find out. Record yourself reading aloud this paragraph.

> Last June, Veronica and Greg moved to New York. She was interested in studying Spanish at a four-year college, and he wanted to get a job. Veronica had already applied to some colleges and universities, so she started school right away and really liked her classes. But Greg had trouble with his job search. He looked at job listings in newspapers and even used Internet job lists for months. Some people at Veronica's school said that local libraries could be good sources of information, but nothing helped Greg. They started to think he would never find something. Finally, after a year, he found a job in one of the offices at Veronica's college. Now, he works right on campus, and in between her classes Veronica meets him for lunch.

Which sounds in this paragraph did you have difficulty saying?

Source: *Sound Concepts* by M. Reed and C. Michaud, 2005, McGraw-Hill. Used with permission.

WRITING DIAGNOSTIC ─────────────────────────────

Ask yourself these questions:

1. From their writing, what do you know students can do?
2. From their writing, what do you know they cannot yet do?

Use one column for each of your students, numbering their writing samples or adding student initials to each column to keep track of them. Use one row for each feature (or error) you notice in their writing. A few sample rows are shown on page 43, but you may tailor these to the level of your students. Check which samples show evidence of each feature or error.

	1	2	3	4	5	6	7	8	9	10
Begins sentences with capital letters and ends sentences with periods.										
Use third-person singular present tense verb endings correctly.										

METACOGNITIVE DIAGNOSTIC

Thinking about Listening and Speaking

Section A: Sound Concepts

1. Native speakers use dictionary ("correct") pronunciations in conversation.
   Agree ◀——▶ Disagree

2. How acceptable are contractions (such as *can't*) in everyday speech?
   Completely acceptable ◀——▶ Somewhat acceptable ◀——▶ Not acceptable (careless speech)

3. How acceptable are shortened forms (such as *gonna*) in everyday speech?
   Completely acceptable ◀——▶ Somewhat acceptable ◀——▶ Not acceptable (careless speech)

4. When I listen to English speakers, I can understand the individual words even if a speaker doesn't exaggerate the space between words.
   Very well—All the time ◀——▶ Somewhat—Sometimes ◀——▶ Not at all—Never

5. When speaking, I link or connect one word to another.
   Very well—All the time ◀——▶ Somewhat—Sometimes ◀——▶ Not at all—Never

Section B: Rhythm & Music

1. How well can I explain the differences between English and my language in syllable structure?
   Very well ◀——▶ Not so well ◀——▶ I never thought about it

2. How important is it to say the correct number of syllables in a word?
   Very important ◀——▶ Somewhat important ◀——▶ Not very important

3. How important is it to use correct stress in words?
   Very important ◀——▶ Somewhat important ◀——▶ Not very important

4. If I can understand every word in a sentence, then I've understood the meaning of the sentence.
   Agree ◀——▶ Disagree

5. In general, intonation doesn't change the meaning of individual English words. Therefore, it's not essential to clear communication.
   Agree ◀——▶ Disagree

6. Intonation and stress change the meaning of sentences.
   Agree ◀——▶ Disagree

7. English questions use rising intonation.
   Always ◀——▶ Sometimes ◀——▶ Never

8. When I read aloud, I know which words to stress and why.
   Agree ◀——▶ Disagree

9. English has a standard pattern of stress, intonation, and timing.
   Agree ◀——▶ Disagree

10. I can tell when a speaker uses non-standard stress or intonation.
    Agree ◄───► Disagree

11. I understand the meaning of non-standard stress and intonation.
    Agree ◄───► Disagree

12. Most English speakers will pause in the same places when reading aloud the same sentence or passage.
    Agree ◄───► Disagree

13. When I read aloud, I think about: (check all that apply)

vowel sounds	consonant sounds
stress	intonation
pauses	thought groups
pronunciation of new words or proper nouns	number of syllables in words

14. *True or false?* Intonation, stress, and timing can. . .
    a. ☐ turn a statement into a question.
    b. ☐ change the meaning of a sentence.
    c. ☐ turn a sincere statement into a sarcastic one.
    d. ☐ reduce the number of words needed to convey your meaning.
    e. ☐ act as oral punctuation, quotation marks, and paragraph breaks.
    f. ☐ convey information without actually saying the words.
    g. ☐ signal an implied contrast.

15. I use clues from a speaker's intonation and stress to help understand a speaker's meaning.
    Always ◄───► Sometimes ◄───► Never

16. I use clues from a speaker's facial expressions and body language to help understand the speaker's meaning.
    Always ◄───► Sometimes ◄───► Never

17. One of the main reasons I have trouble understanding English speakers is that they speak too quickly. If they slowed down, I think I could understand them.
    Agree ◄───► Disagree

Section C: Grammar Sounds

1. Verb and noun endings are unnecessary: words like *yesterday* or *many* already give us the same information.
   Agree ◄───► Disagree

2. The *-s* or *-es* ending on regular third-person singular present tense verbs has different pronunciations.
   Agree ◄───► Disagree

3. Pronouncing the regular past-tense ending (*-ed*) correctly means always adding an extra syllable, *-ed*, onto the verb.
   Agree ◄───► Disagree

4. I use correct verb and noun endings when I speak to teachers.
   Always ←→ Sometimes ←→ Almost never

5. I use correct verb and noun endings when I speak to my peers.
   Agree ←→ Disagree

6. I use correct verb and noun endings when I speak outside of class.
   Agree ←→ Disagree

7. How important is it to use correct verb and noun endings in everyday speech?
   Very important ←→ Somewhat important ←→ Not important

8. My teacher will correct my pronunciation every time I make a mistake.
   Agree ←→ Disagree

9. Whose responsibility is it to keep track of my pronunciation errors?
   My teacher's ←→ Mine

10. I keep a list or a logbook of my pronunciation errors.
    Agree ←→ Disagree

Section D: Consonant & Vowel Sounds

1. How important is the correct pronunciation of consonant and vowel sounds?
   Very important ←→ Somewhat important ←→ Not very important

2. How well can I explain differences between English and my language in vowel sounds?
   Very well ←→ Not so well ←→ I never thought about it

3. Compared to the number of English vowel *letters*, there are _____ English vowel *sounds*.
   Many more ←→ About the same number of ←→ Fewer

4. If I can correctly pronounce all the consonant and vowel sounds, my listeners will understand me.
   Agree ←→ Disagree

5. My biggest pronunciation problems are consonant or vowel sounds.
   Agree ←→ Disagree

6. I feel strange forming some consonant or vowel sounds.
   Agree ←→ Disagree

7. Sometimes, correct pronunciations feel so strange to me that I prefer my own pronunciations.
   Agree ←→ Disagree

Section E: Errors and Change

1. List your biggest pronunciation problems here:

2. What's one strategy you're using to improve your specific pronunciation problems?

3. I know I make pronunciation errors, but I want to improve my speech, not change it.
    Agree ◄──► Disagree

4. *Complete the sentence by choosing the item that best fits the way you feel:*
    There are some things I always get wrong,
    a. ☐ and I know this because my teachers correct me again and again on the same mistakes.
    b. ☐ but, when my teachers say I get the pronunciation "right," it feels so strange and wrong that I think they can't be right.
    c. ☐ but I think I'm saying things the same way my teachers do, so I don't understand where my mistakes are.
    d. ☐ and I'm working on them: I know where my specific mistakes are, and I know how to fix them.

5. If people understand me when I speak, I don't need to make changes to my pronunciation.
    Agree ◄──► Disagree

6. I want to improve my pronunciation.
    Agree strongly ◄──► Agree somewhat ◄──► Disagree

7. I know what changes I need to make to my speech in order to improve.
    Agree strongly ◄──► Agree somewhat ◄──► Disagree

8. I monitor my speech to make these changes and corrections.
    Agree strongly ◄──► Agree somewhat ◄──► Disagree

9. I know when I've been able to successfully change part of my pronunciation.
    Agree strongly ◄──► Agree somewhat ◄──► Disagree

REFLECTIVE JOURNAL

What are your feelings on the formal diagnostics—and ideas for informal diagnostics—presented in this chapter? How do you plan on identifying the language needs of your next group of students?

Consider this case study:

CASE STUDY: YELLOW vs. JELLO ———————————————

Setting: "Jeopardy"-type in-class contest.
  Class divided into two teams, each determined to win.
  The tie-breaking moment:

My student teacher:	*The color of the sun...*
First student to answer:	*What is jello?*
My student teacher:	*You win!!!*
Student teacher debrief:	*Oh, I know what she meant...*

What's the problem here? What does this exchange tell you about teacher accommodation in response to student errors? How can you guard against this problem?

CHAPTER 3

Moving Beyond Choosing the Right Activities

Think about it

What's your image of an ESL teacher? What comes to mind when you try to complete the sentence, *"An ESL teacher is . . ."*?

Chapter 3 includes these topics:

- ☑ Creating lesson plans vs. lesson sequences
- ☑ Understanding the teacher's role in goal-driven lesson planning
- ☑ Revitalizing the ESL tutoring session
- ☑ Seeing goal-driven lesson planning at a glance
- ☑ Assessing lesson plans: A checklist
- ☑ Using a lesson-planning template: Scripting the language of instruction

Creating Lesson Plans vs. Lesson Sequences

REFLECTIVE JOURNAL

Where does lesson planning fit into your image of the ideal ESL teacher's role? What is lesson planning? What does it mean to make a lesson plan? When would you as a teacher make a lesson plan, and who is a lesson plan for?

In most cases, teachers think they know what lesson planning is. Some teachers think they're already doing it: they set aside a certain number of minutes to cover a specific topic or review a specific chapter, and they plan in advance which activities they're going to use. Such planning for the sequence of the lesson is necessary—after all, you need to know what you're going to do at various points in the lesson/tutoring session, what materials you'll need, and what activities students will engage in. But this is not lesson planning. Furthermore, if teachers merely make a list of topics or chapters that they intend to cover or teach from, such a list best approximates a syllabus and is not a true lesson plan.

Other teachers think that lesson planning is unnecessary: it's just something to do when being observed, to satisfy administrative requirements, or only for teachers in more academic contexts. The term *lesson planning* as used here is distinguished from any specific administrative requirements or designated formatting. In fact, a true lesson plan doesn't necessarily have to be written at all. More important than the format is the content: a true lesson plan contains specific measurable, operationalized learning objectives for students. While some teachers may distinguish between their statements of students' objectives and what they call a formal "lesson plan," a lesson plan is defined here primarily through its objectives: in other words, what will students be able to say or do at the end of the lesson? (Some teachers call these SWABTs: **S**tudents **W**ill **B**e **A**ble **T**o.) This type of goal-driven lesson planning is advantageous for teachers and tutors in all contexts, from one-on-one sessions to academic classrooms: it will help your students achieve meaningful and long-lasting language change.

The bottom line in lesson planning is: Shift the focus from you as teacher. Don't describe your behavior—describe **students'** behaviors.

 Eye-Opener

> What many teachers think is a lesson plan is really a *lesson sequence.*

A New View: Lesson Sequences vs. Goal-Driven Lesson Plans

Lesson Sequences	Goal-Driven Lesson Plans
focus on immediate student wants/interests	focus on longer-term student needs
include assessment only as an afterthought, at best	contain built-in assessment
include varied activities for high level of student interest	include activities to advance students toward goals
approach each lesson as an individual event	approach lessons cumulatively
remind teachers what to do in the classroom and when	remind teachers when and why to do things
draw on declarative knowledge	draw on procedural knowledge
use teachers' administrative functions	use teachers' executive functions
consider moment-to-moment tactics	consider overall strategies

SPOTLIGHT ON RESEARCH

Understanding by Design (Wiggins and McTighe, 2005) offers a somewhat similar distinction, distinguishing the teacher's expanded, strategic role in planning as "thinking like an assessor" rather than merely "thinking like an activity designer." This standards-based approach to lesson planning and curriculum design has been popular in the K–12 world for quite awhile; we extend its application to the ESL classroom at any level.

Understanding the Teacher's Role in Goal-Driven Lesson Planning

Teachers are naturally focused on themselves, their role in the classroom, why they entered the field, and the changes they'll bring about in students, among other reasons. One study (Block, 1992) found that ESL teachers have by and large rejected the image of themselves as the "delivery teacher" and now alternate between thinking of themselves in the roles of "**contracted professionals and supportive parents.**" Another study (Guerrero and Villamil 2000) found that ESL teachers tend to use these nine images to define themselves: "co-operative leader, provider of knowledge, challenger/agent of change, nurturer, innovator, provider of tools, artist, repairer, gym instructor [i.e., coach]."

Some teachers think of themselves as students' friends, but in the classroom, teachers need to give students more than friendship. Others think of themselves as students' fairy godmothers (or godfathers), effortlessly changing students' lives, while still others think of themselves as an energetic facilitator or event planner whose main job is to get students talking. Another common image is that of the teacher as encyclopedia—the source of all knowledge. Finally, the image of a teacher as a parent is also a common one: both roles include some drudgery and some rewards, and both involve making the children or students independent of you.

Depending on your image of what it means to be an ESL teacher, you will have different reactions to the idea of goal-driven lesson planning.

Possible Objections to Goal-Driven Lesson Planning

- Artistic, creative teachers may feel that goal-driven lesson planning cramps their style: they see themselves as more creative or spontaneous.

- Teachers focused on being students' friends may not like to consider themselves anything other than students' peers, and setting specific goals and monitoring progress toward those goals might interfere with their self-image.

- Other teachers may think that goal-driven lesson planning is unglamorous and time-consuming, and they may simply not want to have to deal with lesson plans and assessments.

Advantages of Goal-Driven Lesson Planning

- It is a map: you not only know where you're going but also where you're taking the students.
- It's doable: you know you'll be able to meet students' needs.
- You've got a manageable, cumulative task that leads to observable outcomes and measurable, not subjective, assessment.
- After an initial investment in planning, it is less time-consuming over the course of a semester.
- You satisfy all administrative and record-keeping requirements.
- You can use any personal style you wish in the classroom (creative, spontaneous, etc.).

The Teacher's Expanded Strategic Role

Most of the teacher training literature for language teachers primarily describes the role of the teacher as choosing varied and interesting activities, encouraging students to use the target language, and creating a positive classroom atmosphere and relationship with students. These elements are necessary, but not sufficient, for a classroom in which genuine student progress can be made. All of the decisions that go into what teachers commonly think of as lesson planning are instead important decisions that are referred to as the process of **lesson sequencing**. However, teachers cannot make these decisions for their own sakes: the choice of activities and the creation of a positive learning environment must be in service of specific language goals.

In true **goal-driven lesson planning,** the teacher is more than merely an event planner or entertainer; the teacher is a goal-setter who is able to diagnose students' language needs, articulate specific, student-centered language goals, and create activities and a learning environment that advance student progress toward these language goals.

This model provides models of fluency and input in the target language and manages the time, space, and interpersonal dynamics of a classroom. Also, in this model, teachers work at a strategic level and

1. diagnose student needs (needs-analysis)
2. set specific language goals as a result of these needs
3. plan and sequence the activities of the classroom to advance goals
4. monitor and assess student progress toward these goals
5. explicitly inform students of their needs, goals, and progress toward the goals at every step of the way.

Revitalizing the ESL Tutoring Session

1. Define your goals.

2. Make goals clear to students.

3. Give students language to talk about goals.

It's possible to set specific language goals for students even within the confines of a tutoring session. Lesson plans are not just for formal academic classes.

> Think about it: Why are we here? What are our goals?
> What are we trying to give our students?
>
> We all like to talk with students. But recall the difference between being a tutor or teacher and being a conversational partner: **talking isn't teaching.**

To get more out of tutoring sessions, develop a teaching plan and then follow through.

1. In group tutorials, put the daily agenda on the blackboard.
2. Save and refer back to the "what we did" records from large easel pads or your notes.
3. Use metalinguistic terms (*syllables, stress, nouns, verbs, paragraphs,* etc.) when they help students.
4. Be explicit about your purpose ("We're doing this because…").
5. Be realistic. Where are your students now, and what do they really need?
6. Be aware: how much are they *really* getting from the current lesson?

When working one-on-one or in small groups in a tutoring situation, there often is no clearly visible endpoint—no end of the semester, final at the end of a course, etc. It's important, therefore, to pick a date in the future that is meaningful (when your tutee is applying for a new job or educational program) or arbitrary (one month from now, etc.) and then use the goal-driven lesson planning section of this book (pages 56–61) to imagine the objectives to accomplish at the end of this period. From there, work backward with your plan.

It's also possible to not focus on a given endpoint but to always have in mind a set of important, recurrent grammatical or pronunciation points or structures (for example, plural count nouns, past tense endings, etc.). So, what you discuss in a given week is very flexible—whatever reading material you think is interesting, whatever your tutee has going on in his or her life at the moment—but it's always possible to return to the recurrent teaching points.

Examples of how goal-driven lesson plans can function in informal/tutoring situations follow.

Example 1

Setting: Two-hour ESL conversation group, run on a drop-in basis, with 5–20 students of varying abilities

Preparation: an initial topic/prompt for conversation as well as a backup

> *How did your parents meet?*
> *What does your name mean? How did you get the name you have?*
> *What's a common story told to children in your country?*

Goals: Every student will introduce himself or herself and hold the floor for at least two minutes.

Students will form common classroom questions correctly (*How do you spell that?* vs. *How to spell?*).

Students will form the *th* sound in *thank you* correctly with their tongue between their teeth.

Example 2

Setting: same as above

Teacher A's "goals" (less effective):

> I want students to learn about Presidents' Day and discuss it. *(Note: This is not a truly operationalized—i.e., measurable and observable—goal. Nevertheless, this is how many teachers do articulate their intentions for a class or tutoring session.)*

Teacher B's goals (more effective):

> I want students to be able to participate in a discussion on a historical topic, listen to others, and respond appropriately. I want them to be able to ask *wh-* questions and answer them in the past tense in order to ask for and provide information. I want them to practice saying the days of the week.

The difference? Both classes might start with a short reading about the holiday for background information, but then Teacher B would review the necessary pronunciation and grammar and provide models. Teacher B would also control the discussion and focus students on the grammar, pronunciation, and pragmatics involved.

Seeing Goal-Driven Lesson Planning at a Glance

1. The End Point: What will my students be able to say/do at the end of the lesson?
2. The Starting Point: Where are they now?
3. The Lesson: How will I get them there?
   Script "teaching talk" for instruction, tell-backs, and assessment
4. Assessment: How will I know when they get it?

Teaching Talk: The succinct, consistent language you use to refer to a pattern.

Tell-Backs: Students' ability to tell back to the teacher or tutor the key grammar point or pattern.

Preparation: Topic/Content

- The topic or content of the lesson will likely be determined by the syllabus or textbook being used in the class.

Example: passive voice
Consider to what extent to follow the textbook. When is it appropriate to cut or supplement? Which exercises should you use, if any, and why?

- Be sure to ascertain the scope of the lesson. How much is to be covered and in what time frame? It is wise to know how each day's lesson fits in to the overall unit because it helps to see how the parts relate to the whole and to gauge how much time is permissible given what has to be covered in a given semester.

Example: You've already reviewed/taught the basic tenses and are in the process of introducing more complex grammar. You have a week of class time for this topic.

Step I: Start at the End (operationalized objectives)

WHAT IS THE OBJECTIVE OF THE LESSON?
START AT THE BOTTOM OF THE PAGE WHEN PLANNING YOUR LESSON.

- State in behavioral terms and from the student perspective.
- Script what your students will say at the end of the lesson.
- Do not describe what you will do.
- Write examples of the sentences students will produce/write.
- Make it integrated (integrated skills):

  Grammar: how is the grammar construction formulated?

  Usage: how/when is the grammar construction used?

  Pronunciation: what are target consonant/vowel sounds? Suprasegmentals? Noun/verb endings?

> Example: For a given set of vocabulary that students have studied, students will form passives correctly (even with irregular past participles) and will use active, not passive, voice for intransitive verbs.

ANTICIPATE ERRORS

What errors do you anticipate students will make? Be prepared.

Refer to *Learner English* (Swann and Smith, 2001) if you don't know what to anticipate.

1. *The children raised in a bilingual home. (use active when should use passive)
2. *I was won the match by my competitor. (use passive when should use active)
3. *He was grown up in New York. (use passive when should use active because verb in this case can't be used transitively)
4. *It was prove that the facts were wrong. (misforming the passive—*to be* + simple form of verb)

Language-specific considerations:

1. Chinese: topic/comment → pseudo passives (overuse of things that seem like passive)
2. Japanese: adversity passive (overuse of passive)
3. language-specific items that change from passive to active across languages

Step II: From Known to New: What Is the Student Starting Point?

What do the students need to know in order to be able to succeed with the new material?

Example: Passive Voice.
Make sure students know:

- *the difference between a transitive and an intransitive verb*
- *the past participle of irregular verbs, especially those in the target lesson*
- *the pronunciation of regular past participles: [t], [d], [Id]*
- *the conjugations of the verb* to be *for the relevant tenses*

Step III: Concept, Context, and Practice: What Strategy Is Best Suited for the Content?

- inductive: for predictable, rule-governed content (e.g., past tense/ participle allomorphs of regular verbs)
- deductive: for predictable, ruled-governed content (same as for inductive, but takes less time)
- advance organizer: for unpredictable, non-systematic content (e.g., irregular past tense; verbs followed by gerunds or infinitives)
- Plan the theme/topic/context/content students will manipulate
- Plan your activities/ worksheets/ exercises (start with the most controlled → most communicative)

Step IV: Did the Students Learn Anything New? How Will You Know? Focus on What the Students are Saying, Not on What You Are Doing.

- Return to the Lesson Objective(s)
- For each objective there must be a means to know if it was met

Example of assessment: Students will write a paragraph reporting on a neighborhood situation or event of their choice from a list of samples (or an original situation) as though for the local paper. Students will choose the passive in appropriate instances and will form the passives correctly; no intransitive verbs will be used in the passive. They will practice reading their paragraph aloud as though for a radio or TV news report; they will pronounce the three endings of regular past participles correctly. Students will conjugate the verb to be *correctly for tense and number.*

Possible student sentences:

An anonymous contribution was made to the local school.
A young boy's dog was stolen from outside the library.
A rare bird was spotted on the roof of a local apartment building.

Step V: Analyzing the Lesson:
Did You Learn Anything New?
What Will You Do Differently Next Time?

REFLECT ON THE LESSON. MAKE NOTES FOR NEXT TIME.

Unexpected Questions	How I responded	What to do next time

Unexpected Errors/ Problems	How I responded	What to do next time

Step VI: Did the Students Learn Anything New? How Will You Know?

How will you know:

- if the students learned what you taught them?
- if your lesson was a success?

Focus on what the students are saying, not on what you are doing.

- Return to the Lesson Objective(s)
- For each objective there must be a means to know if it was met

Step VII: Analyzing the Lesson:
Did *You* Learn Anything New?
What Will You Do Differently Next Time?

Obviously you will not be able to complete this section since the lesson on *there is/there are* is merely hypothetical at the moment. However, here are some possible examples of notes that you might make, post-lesson, to yourself in the future:

> Unexpected question from student:
>   (in response to Q: Is there a _____? A: Yes, there are three _____s.) "Shouldn't the answer be, 'No, there are three _____s'?"
>
> Unexpected errors students made in class:
>
>   In my country have desert . . . .
>   In USA it have islands . . . . it has islands.
>   In my town is a bridge.

Return to the beginning of your lesson planning. Is there a way in which these "unexpected" errors may in fact have been anticipated? What can you do for planning future lessons, now that you have these errors?

Activity: Goal-Driven Lesson Planning Practice

Following the <u>Goal-Driven Lesson Planning</u> Outline (Steps 1–4), plan a lesson on *There is/ There are.*

Step 1: What is the objective of the lesson?

Grammatical Formulation:

Usage:

Pronunciation:

Anticipate Errors

Step 2: What is the Student Starting Point?

Step 3: Concept, Context, Practice

Practice:

Target Vocabulary from textbook pages:

Theme/ Topic/ Context:

Activities/ Worksheets/ Exercises:
Controlled to Context for Meaningful Use of the Language

Assessing Lesson Plans: A Checklist

1. Explicit list of goals/objectives (lesson plan)

> a. Goals are student-focused. *"Students will. . ."* rather than *"Teachers will. . . ."*

> b. Goals are measurable or observable. *"Students will respond to the question 'What's your name?' appropriately and ask an appropriate follow-up question"* rather than *"Students will make progress in introducing themselves."*

> c. Goals are appropriate for student level and knowledge.

2. Specific, ordered list of classroom activities (lesson sequence)

> a. Activities advance stated goals and reveal progress toward the goals
> *Activities provide formal or informal assessment opportunities.*

> b. Activities are achievable
> *Students have all the knowledge and information they need to complete them.*

> c. Activities specify grouping, materials, and duration.

> d. Activities are student-centered and varied.

Remember: Lesson planning is not the process of choosing the activities for the period, deciding what you're going to cover, or allotting time to different classroom elements. Lesson planning is the process of developing specific language goals for students and determining how to get students to those goals.

Using a Lesson-Planning Template: Scripting the Language of Instruction

Target Concept/Pattern: *tell vs. say*

Refer to Figure 4 on page 64 to see the flow of this material.

STEP 1:

What will you say to present this concept/pattern to students?
How will you prompt them to correct errors with this concept/pattern?

Today we're going to talk about the verbs **tell** and **say**. We use both verbs to report speech, but even though they *mean* the same thing, we use them differently.

Your dictionary shows you how to use these verbs: if you look up the word **tell**, it probably says *tell s.o. s.t.,* or *tell s.b. s.t.,* which means "tell someone something" or "tell somebody something."

Tell and **say:** same meaning, different grammar.

tell s.o. s.t.	indirect speech
tell s.o. + *that* + I.C.	indirect speech
say + *that* + I.C.	indirect speech
say, "_____"	direct speech

- Elicit reminder of what "I.C." is—independent clause—or use "full sentence," depending on your previous language use in the classroom.
- Elicit distinction between indirect and direct speech and clarifications of those terms.
- Walk through simple set of examples.
  - Elicit error with *say* (*He said me. . .) and correction.
  - Elicit more examples from class.

John said, "I won the contest!"
John said that he won the contest.
John told me that he won the contest.
John told me the news.

FIGURE 4 ————————————————————————————
Teaching Talk

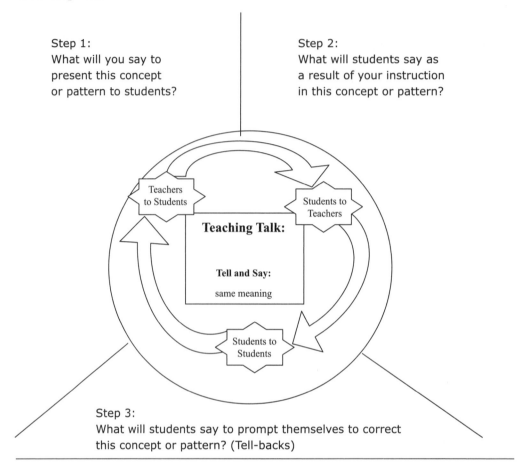

Step 1:
What will you say to
present this concept
or pattern to students?

Step 2:
What will students say as
a result of your instruction
in this concept or pattern?

Teachers
to Students

Students to
Teachers

Teaching Talk:

Tell and Say:

same meaning

Students to
Students

Step 3:
What will students say to prompt themselves to correct
this concept or pattern? (Tell-backs)

STEP 2:

What will students say as a result of instruction in this concept/pattern?
What linguistic goals do you have for your students in this lesson?

- give examples of direct speech using *say* correctly
- change direct speech into indirect (reported) speech using *say* or *tell* correctly
- correct previous errors with *say* and *tell* (example: *He said me. . .)

STEP 3:

What will students say to prompt themselves to correct this concept/pattern?
What metalinguistic goals do you have for your students?

(<u>Note</u>: These are examples of student tell-backs.)

You tell someone something.
You don't say someone.

You tell someone that something is true.
You say that something is true.
You say, "Something. . ."

Tell and *say* have the same meaning, but different grammar.

FIGURE 5

Teaching Talk: A Template

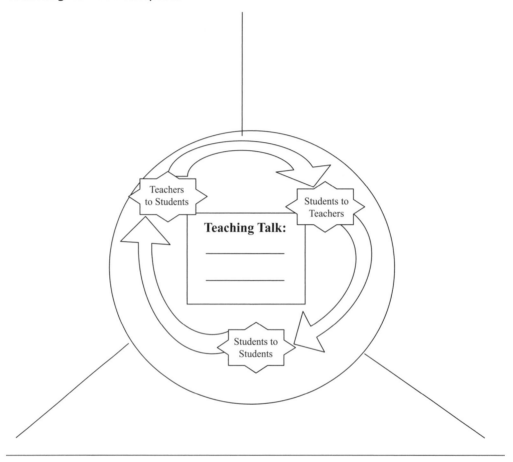

LESSON-PLANNING TEMPLATE: SCRIPTING THE LANGUAGE OF INSTRUCTION

Target Concept or Pattern:

Use Figure 5 on page 66 to plan your own teaching talk.

STEP 1:

What will you say to present this concept/pattern to students?
How will you prompt them to correct errors with this concept/pattern?

STEP 2:

What will students say as a result of instruction in this concept/pattern?
What linguistic goals do you have for your students in this lesson?

STEP 3:

What will students say to prompt themselves to correct this concept/pattern?
What metalinguistic goals do you have for your students?

REFLECTIVE JOURNAL

1. Look back at the sections on goal-driven lesson planning and teacher roles. Write one or two paragraphs describing your (current or projected) English class. Focus on what students will *do* during the class and what students will *be able to do or produce* at the end of the course. This description, which you may choose to share with your students, should contain your overall language goals for the class.

2. Look at these possible statements about lesson planning. Which of them do you think have merit? Why?

    I.   Lesson planning is unnecessary if I'm a talented teacher, good at improvisation, and effective when speaking in front of groups.

    II. Lesson planning is only something you do when you're being observed.

    II. Lesson planning is what you have to do in case you have a substitute or for the administration.

    IV. Lesson planning merely replicates the primary textbook or syllabus, so there's no point to doing it.

    V.   Lesson planning is an exercise teachers do—it has merit in and of itself.

    VI. Lesson planning primarily focuses on activities or materials.

    VII. Lesson planning exists for the sake of keeping track of time or classroom logistics.

    VIII. Lesson planning offers a record of what happened in the class and what students now know.

    IX. Lesson planning concerns what the teacher will do.

3. Think about a lesson in which you were the student (language lesson, sports training session, etc.) and you know you learned something—a time when you were successful with something measurable. Think about the specific goals that your instructor had to get you to that point. What were the components of this task? What were the necessary steps that advanced you toward the goal? Working backward helps you re-create a lesson plan that your instructor may have had in mind. Your feeling of success at the end of the lesson is a real, results-based feeling of success, one that we also want our students to have.

CHAPTER 4

Teaching Language

Imagine that you're in a social setting and meet a new acquaintance who finds out you teach ESL and expresses an interest in pursuing the field as well. What do you say to this person? Think back to your image of a language teacher (as discussed in the Introduction), and think about what, specifically, you think someone needs to know about English to teach it.

This chapter covers these topics:

- ☑ Understanding the elements of teaching ESL: What's required?
- ☑ Moving from implicit to explicit language knowledge: Making sense of typical student errors
- ☑ Moving from explicit knowledge to pedagogical applications: Beyond "It just sounds right that way"
- ☑ Preparing lessons on new (to you) grammar topics
- ☑ Assessing grammar books for classroom use

Understanding the Elements of Teaching ESL: What's Required?

The elements discussed in the Introduction (empathy, activities, goals, organization, and content) are of course necessary for effective teaching. Above all, ESL teachers and tutors teach *language*, but effective ESL/EFL teaching requires knowledge of the language and desire to teach it. If you're reading this book, then you already have demonstrated the desire.

Figure 6 shows what you bring to this task and what this book will help you achieve. Use the figure to analyze the personal abilities and skills that you already possess when entering the classroom. Think back to your list of strengths (page 4). Being comfortable talking in front of groups or being a talented teacher of music or computers are useful attributes that will facilitate your teaching of English, but neither of these personal abilities or skills on their own mean that you can teach your native language.

True comfort and confidence in your teaching doesn't come from what you do—it comes from what your students do as a result of what you do.

FIGURE 6 —————————————————————————————
Three Levels of Linguistic Knowledge

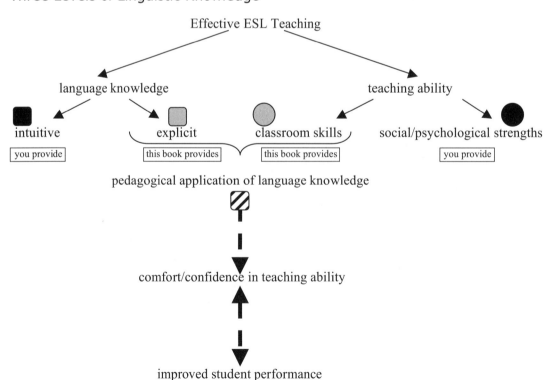

What does it mean to know a language?	Type of Knowledge
1. You can speak the language.	*implicit/linguistic* knowledge of the language
2. You can analyze the language and discern the source of student errors.	*explicit/metalinguistic* knowledge about the language
3. You can explain an error to students in only as much detail as necessary.	*applied pedagogical* knowledge about what students need to produce the language

Teachers bring their own empathy, organization, and language knowledge to the task of teaching. Native speakers of English usually have an unconscious, intuitive knowledge of their own language. Highly proficient nonnative speakers of English already have the conscious, explicit knowledge of English that native speakers need to acquire. Without such explicit (metalinguistic) knowledge of the language, you as teachers will be unable to make sense of some of the most frequent errors students make and understand the source(s) of these errors.

This metalinguistic knowledge—knowledge *about* the language rather than merely of the language—is essential, however, to effectively plan lessons around common student errors or high-frequency grammar topics. Chapter 3 covered goal-driven lesson planning in greater depth. However, explicit and conscious knowledge of the specific grammatical or pronunciation point is a necessary prerequisite to planning any lesson.

Moving from Implicit to Explicit Language Knowledge: Making Sense of Typical Student Errors

Each of the eight items on page 72 includes one of the highest-frequency errors that ESL students tend to make. Some errors will appear more in writing, and some are only apparent in speech. Some errors are more typical of students with one language background than another, and some errors are more typical of students with primarily an aural exposure to English (i.e., students who don't have extensive formal education in English). Making sense of all of these errors, however, requires more than just an intuitive knowledge of English. For each item, talk through answers to these questions and then see pages 73–74.

- Where is the mistake, and how do you correct it?
- How would you describe the mistake to students so that they can avoid making the mistake again? What terms and concepts do you need to draw on to explain why the mistake is wrong and the correct version is right?

1. Yesterday I start-ed school. I walk-ed to the campus. [spoken]

    _____

    _____

2. My friend like Boston. [spoken or written]

    _____

    _____

3. My teacher gave me a lot of advise yesterday. [spoken or written]

    _____

    _____

4. When I came here, I brought three luggages with me. [spoken or written]

    _____

    _____

5. It was occurred. [spoken]

    _____

    _____

6. My sister tecare my kids. [written]

    _____

    _____

7. I like my teacher. Is very friendly. [spoken or written]

    _____

    _____

8. My friend lives in China also studies English. [written]

    _____

    _____

ANSWERS

Error	Explanation
1. Yesterday I start-ed school. I walk-ed to the campus.	This is an error with the regular past tense verb ending. Sometimes, as in the verb *start,* we pronounce the *ed* ending as an extra syllable: we say it [Id], and sometimes we pronounce it as a single sound: we would say it [t] in *walked*, so it should be [walkt]. These different pronunciations are predictable and rule-governed; you need to be able to help students apply the rule to determine when we use which pronunciation.
2. My friend like Boston.	Like Item 1, this is an error with a verb ending—in this case, the third-person singular present tense regular verb ending, *s* (or *ed*). This may be the single most common and intractable error among ESL students. Also as with Item 1, you need to be able to help students apply the rule to determine when the ending is pronounced as a single sound (such as [s] in *likes*) and when as an extra syllable ([Iz] in *watches*).
3. My teacher gave me a lot of advise yesterday.	No, this isn't a spelling error; it's most likely what's commonly known as a word form error—a problem with parts of speech. The student knows the core meaning of *advice/advise* but hasn't paid attention to which form is the noun and which the verb, either in spelling or pronunciation.
4. When I came here, I brought three luggages with me.	Although native speakers don't commonly think of them this way, all nouns in English are either a count noun (we can count them, or make them plural) or a noncount noun (we can't conceive of counting them) or both, depending on the meaning. *Luggage* is a noncount noun—the word relates to the whole concept—while *suitcase* is a count noun and what the student probably wants here. There's no way to know ahead of time which nouns are which—students must simply memorize, for each new noun, whether it's countable or uncountable.
5. It was occurred. [spoken]	In this case, the student was trying to say that something was *awkward*, but she had two suprasegmental pronunciation problems: first, she used incorrect word-level stress, stressing the second syllable instead of the first. Next, she changed the syllable structure of the second syllable as a result of omitting the consonant sound /w/. You need to make sure students understand all of these concepts (syllables, stress, syllable structure) before dealing with this error.

6. My sister tecare my kids. [written]	A Spanish-language L1 student who was illiterate in his native language and who had only recently become literate in English made this error. He wrote the way he spoke—when he read this sentence aloud, he read the odd-looking *word tecare* as three syllables, essentially "take care of," which he'd heard but didn't have the language knowledge to realize was actually three words, without the third-person singular present tense verb ending. To address this error, you'd need to know that the student routinely omits the third-person singular ending when speaking, and you'd need to explicitly focus on all of these aspects of the error.
8. I like my teacher. Is very friendly.	This is an example of a basic sentence-structure error, a missing subject. Many languages in the world are called pro-drop languages, and they allow sentences to be formed with a null or unstated subject if one is readily apparent and implied, as in the example.
8. My friend lives in China also studies English.	This is an example of one type of a large set of more complicated grammatical errors. The student was probably incorrectly forming a relative clause (*My friend who lives in China...*), but may also be confused about the function of the word *also* (it can't act as a conjunction, like *and,* to link two sentence elements); in either case, the resulting sentence looks squashed together, as though there simply are two verbs. Depending on the level of the student, you might advise the student to rephrase the sentence as, *My friend lives in China and studies English* or you might explicitly teach relative clauses. We give you the example of this error not because this one specific error is one of the more frequent or more important mistakes ESL students will make, but as an example of the kinds of errors you will encounter beyond this small, high-frequency set.

Moving from Explicit Knowledge to Pedagogical Applications: Beyond "It Just Sounds Right That Way"

Given these eight errors, intuitive knowledge of English is not sufficient to explain these mistakes and make students able to produce them correctly. Therefore, if you know you are going to cover a specific grammar point, you need to increase your own explicit knowledge of that particular point and from the standpoint of your students: What do the students need to know to correct the error or to understand so they don't make this mistake?

If you have... →	*Then you can...*
Level 1. implicit language knowledge →	find and correct students' mistakes for them
Level 2. explicit language knowledge →	label students' mistakes and explain why they're wrong
Level 3. applied pedagogical knowledge →	give students as much—and only as much—information as they need to know in order to correct this particular mistake and check for this type of error in the future

Teachers or tutors who are at Level 1 of the chart correct the immediate error, help solve communication breakdowns, and facilitate conversation at the moment. In writing, however, this is the function of an editor or proofreader—not a tutor or teacher. In writing or in speech, there is no long-term benefit to the student from teachers working at this level.

Teachers or tutors who are at Level 2 of the chart can explain the mistake and use grammatical terms to label it, but this explanation in itself is not usable by students and will not lead students to avoid this mistake in the future.

Teachers or tutors who are at Level 3 of the chart have planned and thought beyond the immediate moment to where they want students to be in the future—at the end of the class, unit, course, etc. These teachers give students a succinct and consistent explanation of the error (what we call the *teaching talk*) that students can internalize and then repeat back to teachers; students can then correct their particular error, but also have the ability to monitor for and correct other errors of this type in the future.

An example of how to work through these different levels for one particular kind of student error is shown on pages 76–77. A template that you can use to plan lessons on any other kind of student error appears on page 78.

SAMPLE LESSON PLAN
FOR A GRAMMAR MINI-LESSON

Error: **In my country, have a lot of snow. Is cold in winter.**

Correction: In my country, there's a lot of snow. It's cold in winter.
At this point, you are working at the level of an implicit, linguistic, knowledge of English. Your correction of the error solves the immediate conversational difficulty (if there is one), but does not teach the student how to correct that type of error in the future. **Getting students to supply this correct form is your objective.**

Teacher Understanding of Error Source:
   Student may speak a pro-drop or null subject language that allows
      omitted subjects; student doesn't use *there is/there are* (or *it*)
      as existential subjects.
At this point, you are working at the level of an explicit, metalinguistic, knowledge of English. Your understanding of the source of the error is necessary to help you formulate what you will tell students about it. You may need to look at several grammar books to arrive at this point, but you do not yet have a script for teaching students about this error. At this point, however, you can actually write your measurable and observable language-based goals for students:
   At the end of this lesson, students will be able to use the existential *there is/there are* where necessary and appropriate.

Teaching Talk:
   (minimal necessary version of teaching talk)
   Every sentence in English needs a stated subject: use *there is* or *there are* to show something exists.

   (expanded version of teaching talk, with preview-explain-recap)
   Every sentence in English needs a stated subject: use *there is* or *there are* to show something exists.

   Usually, a subject is the person or thing doing the action in a sentence. If there's no action—if you're talking about existence or states—then there's no obvious subject. We call that an empty subject. But remember that every sentence needs a subject! The subject slot can't be empty. Use *it* or *there* to fill the empty subject slot in a sentence. If there's a thing that exists (snow, bookstores, democracy), use *there is* or *there are*.

So remember, every sentence in English needs a stated subject: use *there is* or *there are* to show something exists.

At this point, you are working at the level of an applied pedagogical knowledge of English. Your "teaching talk" is **the minimal necessary explanation of the error for students** *in order for them to avoid making this error in the future—or, at the very least, to correct this error for themselves after a prompt. This succinct, consistent language is your script for teaching students about this error. Use the keywords in your teaching talk (in this example, "we need a subject") to prompt students to correct if they make this error in the future. Students need to internalize your teaching talk and use the keyword prompts to self-monitor for this error.*

TEMPLATE FOR LESSON PLANNING: GRAMMATICAL MINI-LESSONS

Error: _____

Correction: _____

*At this point, you are working at the level of an implicit, linguistic, knowledge of English. Your correction of the error solves the immediate conversational difficulty (if there is one), but does not teach the student how to correct that type of error in the future. **Getting students to supply this correct form is your objective.***

Teacher Understanding of Error Source:

_____

_____

_____

_____

At this point, you are working at the level of an explicit, metalinguistic, knowledge of English. Your understanding of the source of the error is necessary to help you formulate what you will tell students about it. You may need to look at several grammar books to arrive at this point, but you do not yet have a script for teaching students about this error.

Teaching Talk:

_____

_____

_____

_____

*At this point, you are working at the level of an applied pedagogical knowledge of English. Your "teaching talk" is **the minimal necessary explanation of the error for students** in order for them to avoid making this error in the future—or, at the very least, to correct this error for themselves after a prompt. This succinct, consistent language is your script for teaching students about this error. Circle the keywords in your teaching talk above that you will use to prompt students to correct if they make this error in the future. Students need to internalize your teaching talk and use the keyword prompts to self-monitor for this error.*

Terminology Trouble?

Many teachers are reluctant to use specific grammatical terms in the classroom. At times it might be because a term is not familiar to a teacher, but at other times, it might be so as not to overwhelm students with terminology.

While terminology isn't the goal of your grammar lesson, it is often the missing link that helps students gain better control of a grammatical construction. Specific terms can help in these ways:

- A shared classroom terminology means everyone's on the same page: metalanguage helps the classroom run.

- With specific terms, students have a label for each concept—they can slot it into their brains, and file it away.

If students know what a given construction is called, they'll be able to ask specifically about it and even look it up in other grammar books.

Preparing Lessons on New (to You) Grammar Topics

So, how do you arrive at your explicit—and then applied pedagogical—knowledge of a particular aspect of English? These strategies may help.

1. Narrow your goal: your goal isn't to find out everything about this topic. Rather, it's to find out what you need to say to or show students in order for them to successfully correct the error. Without knowing what students need to say or do at the end of the lesson, you don't know what you need to know about this grammar point.

2. Go to the sources. Use grammar reference books, some written specifically for teachers and some for students. Look at how the books introduce this topic and the typical kinds of sentences or examples they present. Think about how students will actually *use* this construction.

3. Simplify your sources. Don't look at every book out there. Try to limit yourself to a manageable number of sources, realizing that in general, most books do contain the same information; it's just presented differently.

4. Decide what's minor vs. what's major. In other words, decide what is essential for students to know in order to be able to produce this construction. Set aside anything that students do not need to worry about right now.

5. Deal with terminology. Find out for yourself what the key terms are in this area and what they mean. Decide which terms are essential for students to know and how you'll define them for students; use terms as tools, not as ends in and of themselves. Match the terms to students' needs and abilities.

6. Internalize the concept. Be able to close the book and describe the concept. At first, this will be wordy and fuzzy; practice until you know this concept cold and are able to repeat an explanation of it succinctly and consistently.

7. Construct your teaching talk. Write the script you will use to present the grammar to students, including any terms you will use, and standardized explanations of them. Your written script doesn't have to be exactly what you will say in the classroom; Chapter 7 discusses how you don't need to script for an entire lesson—only your succinct, minimalist teaching talk for this concept. Rehearse your grammatical presentation, and practice using your script with and without interruptions. Choose the key words from your teaching talk that will be your prompts to students to return to this concept later on, and correct any errors with it.

Assessing Grammar Books for Classroom Use

Examine several grammar and usage books as you prepare to teach a new grammar point. Here are some useful steps.

Part 1—Preview the Book

1. Read the title, subtitle, authors, and publication information. Is the book old or new? Where do the authors teach or work? What does the title suggest about the focus of the book?

2. Look at the back of the book and the To the Teacher (if there is one). What do the publishers and author(s) think are the main advantages of the book? What are the key features? What do you learn about how to navigate through the book?

3. Look at the contents list. How many chapters/units are there, and how long is each one on average? How many class meetings will your course have, and how might this match up to the number of chapters?

4. Think about the organizational principle of the book. What comes first, and why? How necessary is it to complete Chapter/Unit 2, for instance, before Chapter/Unit 3?

5. Flip through the book. What do you notice about the layout, the margins, the types of activities, and the progression of each chapter? What are some recurrent exercise types or features?

6. Choose a specific grammar point to examine closely in the book. For example, you might choose adverbs of frequency or *there is/there are*; choose anything that might appear on a typical syllabus or that you would be required to teach.

   a. Think about where in the book your given topic comes. Is that logical? What comes immediately before and what after?

   b. Use the index (if there is one) to find other references to this topic. Does the book return to this topic (recycling it) later on, or is this one section the only mention of it?

   c. Look at the first introduction to this grammar topic in the book. What metalanguage does the book use to present it? What terms must your students be familiar with in order to make sense of this explanation? Are there any parts of the grammatical explanation that feel overly complex to you? Think about what benefit these complexities could have to offer. Remember that you're not teaching grammar for its own sake: grammatical explanations are only useful to elicit the correct patterns from students and to provide a common language for classroom discussion of the pattern.

   d. Look at the exercises that follow the introduction of your specific grammar topic. Are the exercises open-ended or controlled, and to what extent? Is there a logic to their order? To what extent are the exercises contextualized, providing real and meaningful contexts for use of the patterns? Think about how students would work through these exercises in the classroom. What would you want them to do in pairs, in small groups, or as the whole class, and why? Is there a benefit to "going over" every exercise? Which exercises lead into more open-ended opportunities for practicing the target pattern?

7. Summarize your view of this book. How useful are the organization, the grammatical explanations, and the exercises? To what extent would you want to supplement either the grammatical explanations or the exercises in the classroom, and why?

Now, having built up your applied pedagogical knowledge of the language point, you are ready to think about setting language goals and enabling students to reach them.

Part 2—Examine Individual Exercises

Teachers often find themselves departing from their primary textbook and supplementing with outside activities, downloaded materials, or even just skipping around within a given textbook. In these cases, you'll need to be very careful that both you and your students can be successful with these other activities. For example, every expansion activity may contain vocabulary unfamiliar to your students; you as a teacher need to determine what vocabulary your students will need to know to complete the activity successfully and what is tangential. Use the guidelines to help you, and refer to Chapter 7 for more tips on success with different kinds of activities.

Critical success factors for teachers:

- You have the applied pedagogical knowledge of the underlying language topics.
    - You have used the templates in this chapter, if needed, to advance your knowledge of this topic.
    - You can offer a minimal necessary version of teaching talk.
- You can place this activity within the larger scope of your course/unit.
    - You can differentiate between essential and tangential aspects of the activity at hand.
    - You are able to articulate observable and measurable goals for your students with regard to this activity.

Critical success factors for students:

- Your students have what they need to be successful with this activity, in terms of:
    - language
    - metalanguage
    - background knowledge
    - schema
    - and skills
- Your students will be able to state the point of the activity at the end of it.

REFLECTIVE JOURNAL

As mentioned in this chapter, intuitive language knowledge fails to explain many student errors or communicate the problem to others. How good were you at being able to articulate the language problem for each of the eight errors shown on page 72? Why? How do you characterize your knowledge of English at this point?

Many native speakers of English haven't formally studied grammar, or do not recall anything useful from those lessons if they did. What kind of instruction did you have in grammar? How easy or difficult was it for you to make sense of the errors on page 72 as a result of your grammar or knowledge?

Sometimes, teachers make observations about student errors that are so vague as to be unhelpful to both teacher and student. What, for example, is wrong with these observations about student errors? What level of language knowledge would you say each teacher observation represents?

> My learners tend to drop the s at the ends of words.
> I've noticed that my students pronounce the silent letters.

CHAPTER 5

Responding to Student Errors

Imagine that you're in the classroom after having implemented a goal-driven approach. Your students are working toward measurable and observable language goals; you've used your minimal necessary teaching talk; and you are confident in your goal-driven plan for getting students to the end of the lesson. But there's a problem: despite all of these things, your students are still making mistakes with the language construction you're teaching. What do you do? How do you respond to their errors with the target form?

This chapter covers these topics:

- ☑ Considering a rationale for corrective feedback
- ☑ Reviewing historical approaches to student errors and corrective feedback in SLA
- ☑ Examining current views on corrective feedback
- ☑ Developing a principled approach to corrective feedback
- ☑ Implementing the teacher-student partnership and working toward learner independence

Considering a Rationale
for Corrective Feedback

The situation described is a very common dilemma encountered by teachers. Consider this in relation to the four levels of competence we introduced in Chapter 2:

> Students begin the course making errors, but are not aware of them (Level 1); they can then progress to being aware of their mistakes (Level 2) and from there to consciously correcting them (Level 3). The ultimate goal, of course, is unconscious competence (Level 4), where students automatically produce the correct form (no errors) without thinking about it.

Students cannot progress through these levels with no intervention, and this is where teachers influence learner progress. There must be *some* attention to student errors in order to move students up the ladder, but these must also be an opportunity for students to self-correct (without intervention) (Level 3).

The time to think about how to deal with student errors is *before* you walk in the classroom. When student errors are occurring in real time, you need to be able to rely on a principled approach that you have determined and committed to beforehand. This approach should of course be consistent with—able to be applied to—your goal-driven lesson plans. (See pages 56–61.)

Reviewing Historical Approaches to Student
Errors and Corrective Feedback in SLA

Second language teachers' views of learner errors have evolved over time and have usually been tied to the theoretical frameworks of the day. However, SLA research has also consistently influenced what teachers do in the classroom.

Behaviorism (approximately 1920s–1950s) viewed language acquisition as a result of imitation and habit formation; therefore, teachers tended to use Lado-inspired (audio-lingual) drills that offered minimal latitude for unscripted communication and, therefore, for error.

The Chomskyan Revolution (1957–beyond) viewed errors as a window into psycholinguistic language processing. By the 1980s, many teachers were using a version of a Krashen-inspired communicative approach that allowed free expression—and many errors—with minimal attention to form. (See Corder, S.P., 1967, The significance of learners' errors. *IRAL*, 5, pp. 161–170).

Earlier approaches and drills produced learners who could not effectively communicate, despite near-perfect form in classroom drills, but more recent communicative approaches tended to produce learners who could produce language but who also had communication difficulties because their utterances could be so inaccurate as to strain their listeners.

In the midst of a communicative approach to SLA, teachers were conflicted about how to handle errors in the classroom, as revealed in surveys of teacher attitudes by Allwright and Hendrickson. Allwright (1975) found disagreement in the field regarding what errors to correct and when and how to correct them. Hendrickson (1978) found that, in general, three types of student errors are typically corrected: those that occur frequently, those that impair communication, and those that are stigmatized.

Since our students will be communicating with—and in school or work judged by—native speakers of English, some research has looked at native-speaker reactions to ESL/EFL speech. Teachers may therefore want to focus more heavily on errors that research shows us native speakers object strongly to. For example, Beebe (1978) found that errors are labeled derisively by native speakers as sounding comical, incompetent, and childish. Major (1995) found that the lack of the third-person singular verb ending, in particular, evokes strong negative native-speaker reactions, including views of the speaker as uneducated, low class, and unintelligent. While teachers and students alike may want to ignore such "minor errors" in favor of more advanced structures, becoming aware of such native-speaker reactions shows them the importance of working on these fundamentals as well.

In the last 20 years or so, the current direction of the field of SLA suggests a view of errors as "natural and necessary as well as a valuable indicator of students' progress" (Major, 1988), and as the scales teeter between the extremes of accuracy and fluency, teachers are returning to a balanced view: a focus on form within a communicative approach (Long, 1991; Lightburn & Spade, 1990; Andrews, 2007).

Examining Current Views on Corrective Feedback

Language learners, of course, make errors and don't recognize the errors or understand the source of their errors. Most teachers generally feel the need to address some of the errors, but they are not sure which errors to address or how.

Numerous studies (Panova & Lyster, 2002; Loewen, 2005) have shown that the most common way teachers address errors is to "recast" the student's error in the proper form.

Example:

Learner: I'm a diborce attorney.

Teacher/Tutor: Oh, how interesting. A *divorce* attorney!

Learner: Yes, I handle many diborce cases.

In this example, the learner makes an error with the /b/ and /v/ sounds (common to learners from a variety of language backgrounds, including Japanese and Spanish, among others). The interlocutor responds with a brief content-related comment (*Oh, how interesting.*) and by recasting the student's utterance with the error corrected. In this case, the tutor pointed out the error using contrastive stress (*A divorce attorney!*). However, the learner did not pick up on the corrective intent of the recast and, instead responded to it to show interest and continue speaking.

A conversational partner would indeed want to show interest in the topic of conversation and prompt the learner to continue talking, but a language teacher interested in the pronunciation error would instead want to focus the learner's attention on the error. This exchange does not do that.

There are a number of problems with the use of recasts in the classroom as a means of giving learners feedback on their errors:

- Learners generally do not notice the gap between their inaccurate utterance and the teacher's corrected recast.
- Learners sometimes interpret these recasts as requests for more information, repetitions of their statement for the benefit of their classmates, etc.
- There is no actual language change on the part of learners (in general) after most recasts.

According to one study (Panova & Lyster, 2002), recasts are the most used, but least effective, method of drawing learners' attention to their errors. In addition, many teachers deal with student errors by ignoring them at the moment and then attempting to draw students' attention to them after the fact (*Great, but remember, two sentences ago, when you said. . .*). This strategy is too little, too late, and does not succeed in bringing learners to the point of uptake.

At other times, teachers may try spot corrections. In these cases, when they hear an error, they suddenly provide the accurate form, drawing the student's attention to the error and the entire class's attention to the error. Then they make students repeat the correct form, despite the fact that this error (perhaps a mispronunciation of a proper noun, etc.) may be a random, one-time occurrence. Spot corrections, in general, are not successful because they are not tied to the ongoing work of the course, tend to disrupt the flow of the class, and do not lead to lasting language change for students (uptake).

Many ESL students we have talked to over the years say that they want to make progress in their language skills. Generally speaking, students are incapable of being more specific: they don't really know what progress looks like, and they don't know specifically how to get there or when they've arrived.

STUDENTS SAY...

"I want to improve my English."
"I want to make more progress."
"I want to get more exposure to English."
"I want to think in English without translating."

BUT IN ORDER TO REACH THESE VAGUE GOALS, STUDENTS PLAN TO...

study more
watch more TV/movies in English
learn a specific number of new vocabulary words
learn more grammatical rules and patterns
make friends with English speakers

Teachers must be more specific, more concrete, and less accommodating than our students are. Teachers need to think about students' language needs well beyond the classroom and to focus on the specific, often repetitive and unglamorous inaccuracies of students' daily speech.

If a teacher's goals and plans for students merely replicate students' unformed goals and undirected plans for themselves, teachers aren't bringing anything to the task. Furthermore, if teachers provide nothing beyond what is offered in a textbook, they also are not adding value to the classroom. One way to value is to intervene and draw students' attention to their errors; if we can get students to the point of uptake—noticing their errors and self-correcting them—then we can move students up the ladder of the levels of competence.

Developing a Principled Approach to Corrective Feedback

What does work is having a principled approach to dealing with learner errors, one that is thought through ahead of time, before the need for spot corrections arises, and that is consistent with the language-based goals of your course. It also is consistently and cumulatively implemented throughout the course.

The analogy of saving a document in a word-processing program represents why we think tying error feedback to the goals of the course is so essential.

The Word Processing Analogy and Noun and Verb Endings

Students typically make two types of errors with regular nouns and verbs: they fail to produce the endings in spontaneous speech and reading aloud, and they mispronounce/over-supply the extra syllable ending.

---

1. On a computer, you create a new file and enter information into it.

After instruction and succinct teaching talk, students "create" or "open" a mental document to remember when/how to pronounce noun and verb endings.

Example: the three ways to pronounce the past tense of regular verbs (or the plural of count nouns, etc.)

2. You have to give your word processing file a name in order to save it and find the information again.

In their notes, students label the rule for when to produce the ending and how to pronounce it.

Example:
Count Noun Plural
Past Tense Regular } 3 pronunciations

3. When you want to find the information again on your computer, you find the file by name and open it.

When your students make a mistake after the rule has been introduced, match your feedback prompt to your teaching talk.

Example: Count Noun Plural?
This prompts the student to mentally "click twice, open the document, read the rule."

A Systematic Approach to Corrective Feedback: Introduction to the Corrective Feedback Flow Chart

Students make so many errors—how do I know which errors to correct?

Do not correct any errors until you have introduced the concept or sound in class.

Students must be able to refer back to something in order to successfully process your correction, or else your correction will go in one ear and out the other.

Students need to have a label, a name, for their pronunciation mistakes. *(refer to the analogy)*

Only when students understand the specific kind of mistake they made will they be able to correct it themselves in the future. Therefore, bringing students' attention to problems that they are not yet able to name will not result in lasting changes to their pronunciation.

A Systematic Approach to Corrective Feedback: A Teacher-Student Partnership

Error correction is most effective when students themselves correct their error, rather than when teachers merely recast it for them. Use the following steps to help students correct their own errors:

1. **Stop**—Stop students mid-utterance when they make errors that have already been addressed.
2. **Find**—When students are new to this process, you might need to point out where in their utterance the error is. Soon students should be able to mentally rewind and find their errors for themselves.
3. **Correct**—Require that students always correct their own errors; even if you (or the students' classmates) have already offered the correct form—in the form of recasts, etc.—the student who made the mistake must accurately repeat the correct form (before continuing with his or her original utterance).
4. **Freeze**—Tell students immediately when they have said the correct form. This "freeze-frame" lets students create a motor-memory of their pronunciation, and leads to a change in their acoustic image of the sound.

The flowchart on page 92 shows this process in more detail.

A Systematic Approach to Corrective Feedback: The Teacher-Student Partnership in Action—Moving Students through the Four Levels of Competence

The flowchart here shows this process in great detail, and the one on page 93 shows it in slightly less detail. You may want to share this chart with students so that they are clear on the process of error feedback in your course.

FIGURE 7

A Principled Approach to Corrective Feedback (for Teachers)

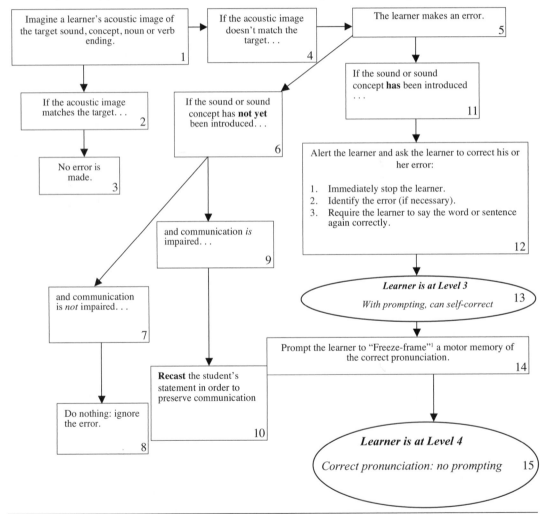

[1] Why do we need the freeze-frame? "Even if [students] do succeed in producing the target sound, there is no unambiguous way for students to mark and remember the sound they produced so that they can reproduce it on their own. Usually they are left with an abstract phonetic symbol or a vague internal feeling of how to make the sound" (Arlington, 1993/94).

Source: *Sound Concepts* by M. Reed and C. Michaud, 2005, McGraw-Hill. Used with permission.

A Principled Approach to Corrective Feedback: A Teacher-Student Partnership

Figure 8 shows what the process of moving through the four levels of competence looks like.

FIGURE 8 ─────────────────────────────────

A Principled Approach to Corrective Feedback (for Students)

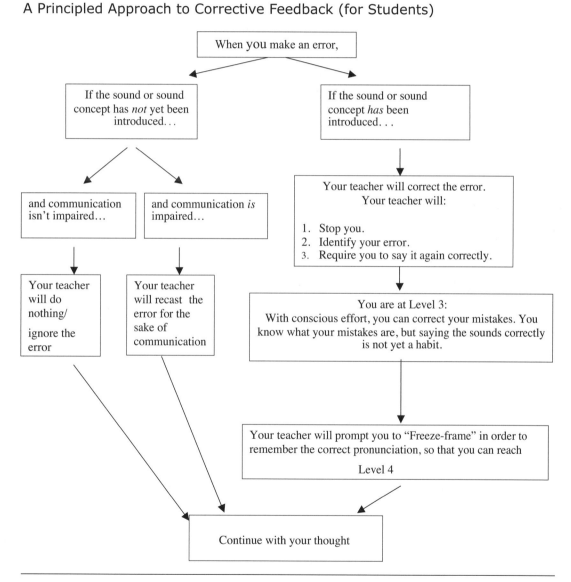

Source: *Sound Concepts* by M. Reed and C. Michaud, 2005, McGraw-Hill. Used with permission.

How (Specifically) Should You Offer Feedback on Students' Errors?
Figure 8 says that when a learner makes an error with a target form, you should:

1. Immediately stop the learner.
2. Identify the error (if necessary).
3. Require the learner to say the word or sentence again correctly.

Often, teachers who have not seen this process in action have trouble imagining how it might play out in a classroom. First, note that it's most important to simply get learners to say the correct form; it's less important *how* you get learners to say it. Some examples of how different types of error feedback might work are given.

■ Recast
   Learner: Today is Friday. Every Friday Luis go to the bank—
   Teacher: Luis goes to the bank.

■ Explicit correction
   Learner: Today is Friday—every Friday Luis go to the bank—
   Teacher: Not *go*—*goes.*

■ Clarification Request
   Learner: Today is Friday—every Friday Luis go to the bank—
   Teacher: Sorry? He what?

■ Elicitation
   Learner: Today is Friday—every Friday Luis go to the bank—
   Teacher: Every Friday Luis. . . .

■ Repetition
   Learner: Today is Friday—every Friday Luis go to the bank—
   Teacher: Luis *go* to the bank?

■ Metalinguistic
   Learner: Today is Friday—every Friday Luis go to the bank—
   Teacher: Third-person singular?

In all cases, we would hope that the final step in this dialogue—the student's uptake—would be something like this.

> *Learner:* Oh, Luis *goes* to the bank to cash his check.

In other words, it does not matter what kind of feedback you offer on a student's error as long as you offer feedback. What counts is the student's uptake.

Earlier we addressed a common teacher concern of feeling incapable of focusing on accuracy and meaning at the same time (see page 27). You *can* do both—you should be particularly attuned to listening for errors with the sounds or patterns that you are monitoring for. You should always be focusing on your students' intent, the meaning they are trying to convey. You also need to be narrowly focused on the actual *content* of their utterances. With a very clear focus on a short list of errors that you will be monitoring for and students will be held accountable for, filter out the random errors with untaught structures and new pronunciations and focus only on the select list of patterns you are targeting for accuracy.

Implementing the Teacher-Student Partnership and Working toward Learner Independence

More will be discussed in Chapters 7 and 8 about tools that will help manage the logistics and record-keeping tasks of the goal-driven classroom, but here we focus on the theory of the teacher-student partnership. This means working to make our learners not need us anymore, to be independent of us. Teachers cannot do the work for the learners, and learners (in general) cannot move to the point of independence without teacher help. Make this idea of the teacher-student partnership transparent to your students. Some ideas that will help you in this endeavor follow.

Teacher Logs: The Teacher-Student Partnership in Action

Whatever form of log your students use to keep track of their errors, keep a corresponding list of selected items that you are helping students master. Create a cumulative log for each class you teach.

The log may be very simple and brief. It is no more than a reminder for you of what errors you are helping students monitor. You should be able to easily recall the items on your log for a given class.

<u>Example</u>: Teacher log for intermediate speaking/pronunciation class

1. Third-person singular verb endings
2. Past tense verb endings (also in participles and passives)
3. Count noun plural endings
4. Possessive noun endings
5. Correct word-level stress in target vocabulary words
6. Contrastive stress where appropriate

HELPFUL HINT

Write a brief version of this list for each class on a large piece of posterboard, and display it on an easel at the front of your room. Use any logistical means appropriate for your room setup (an electronic slide projected on a screen, some standard-sized cards with large letters that you tape/tack around your room, etc.). This way both you and your students can easily and quickly see the list of errors you are monitoring for.

If you don't have such a list—or even before you get the posterboard out for the day—you may want to quickly ask students to list the basic errors that you are monitoring for. Students should be able to do this—as a class, they should be able to come up with the list together quite quickly. If they can, you will see that you have successfully made the process of error feedback transparent to your students.

If you are teaching an integrated skills class or an ESL writing class, you may still want to include pronunciation instruction in the classroom. If so, use the same teacher-student partnership (principled approach to corrective feedback, student logbooks, checklists, and teacher logs) to help students with their pronunciation.

<u>Example</u>: Teacher log for advanced writing class

1. Third-person singular verb endings
2. Past tense verb endings (also in participles and passives)
3. Count noun plural endings (with no articles in front when used for things in general)
4. Possessive noun endings
5. Correct word-level stress in target vocabulary words
6. Contrastive stress where appropriate (especially when reading aloud italicized words)

Follow the same principles for constructing a teacher log of errors for core ESL classes.

A template for helping students keep track of their (in this case) speaking errors is shown. Note that once you've introduced the concept of a student error log, it does not take time away from classroom instruction. You can simply direct a student to add or refer to an entry in his or her logbook as the need arises. The log on page 98 is written to the student and can serve as a model.

The Teacher-Student Partnership in Action: Tools for Moving to Level 2

Use a log to help you enter mistakes, label them by kind, and review a list of *your* biggest problems. If you keep making the same kinds of errors, use your log to help you correct them.

Everyone has different pronunciation problems. Look at the examples on the chart to see the different difficulties three students had with the same word. To improve, students need to know what their individual mistakes are.

Word or Phrase	How should I say it?	How did I say it?	What was my mistake?	Other Examples
Student 1: speech	speech (1 syllable)	su-peech (2 syllables)	separating the first two consonants	su-trong/strong
Student 2: speech	speech (1 syllable)	es-peech (2 syllables)	adding a vowel sound at the front	es-port/sport
Student 3: speech	speech (1 syllable)	speech-ee (2 syllables)	adding a vowel sound at the end	each-ee/each

HINTS ON USING YOUR LOG

- *How should you use your log?* You can use your logbook at any time to enter problems or mistakes. Different students will enter problems at different times.

- *When should you use your log?* When you notice that a specific sound or concept is a problem for you, enter it in your logbook. Remember, the first step in fixing mistakes is noticing where the mistakes are. You need to be an active listener in class. Notice when your teacher corrects you or classmates can't understand you. These might be signals that you should enter that sound or concept in your logbook.

■ *Why should you use your log?* Your logbook is a tool to help you pay more attention to these mistakes. Using your logbook will help you make progress from Level 3, Conscious Competence, to Level 4, Unconscious Competence.

The Teacher-Student Partnership in Action: Tools for Moving to Level 2

Use a log to help you enter mistakes, label them by kind, and review a list of *your* biggest problems. If you keep making the same kinds of errors, use your log to help you correct them.

Everyone has different pronunciation problems. Use this chart to write the words you have difficulty with. Write the correct pronunciation, your error, and how to correct your mistakes.

Word or Phrase	How should I say it?	How did I say it?	What was my mistake?	Other Examples

REFLECTIVE JOURNAL

These teacher-student interactions show student errors and teacher feedback. Errors were corrected in real time, and only after instruction on the target form had taken place.

Set A

> *S1:* The author claim …
>
> *T:* No
>
> *S1:* The author claim …
>
> *T:* Third-person singular
>
> *S1:* I know. I always make that mistake.

Set B

> *S2:* The author claim …
>
> *T:* No
>
> *S2:* The author claim …
>
> *T:* Third-person singular
>
> *S2:* Everyone understand me.

Set C

> *S3:* In this enwironment …
>
> *T:* No
>
> *S3:* In this enwironment …
>
> *T:* V
>
> *S3:* I know. In my country we don't have this sound.

Set D

> *S4:* The author say . . . says that . . .

What can we, as teachers, conclude from this? How do the levels of competence help you make sense of these examples? What are some of the differences among the students' responses, and what do those differences suggest about the level of students?

Given these examples and the information in this chapter, what is your philosophy about error correction? What will your plan for error feedback be when you enter your classroom? Will your plans vary by class, content, level, and point in the semester? How?

CHAPTER 6

Assessing Student Progress

Think about it

Imagine that you suddenly are asked to pick up an extra class the day before the semester starts. Even though you have never taught the level before, you are handed the book on your way into the room on the first day. You make it through the first week or two of the course, getting a feel for the students, the level, and the book. You may even have discrete language goals for your students for individual lessons, but by the end of the first two weeks, you realize that something is missing: This is a graded class, and you realize that you need to be giving students some kind of (in this case) graded assessment in order to track their progress. What do you do? How do you come up with your assessment plan, and what do you think you should do differently the next time you teach a new course?

This chapter will cover these topics:

- ☑ Viewing assessment as the natural outcome of goal-driven lesson planning
- ☑ Understanding the reciprocal nature of language goals and assessment
- ☑ Reconsidering different kinds of assessments and their role in lesson planning
- ☑ Addressing the value and place of assessment in ungraded courses and in tutoring situations
- ☑ Revisiting assessment at the beginning and end of the course

Viewing Assessment as the Natural Outcome of Goal-Driven Lesson Planning

This example is a very realistic situation for many teachers. The teacher's day-to-day lesson plans and individual language goals are the building blocks for assessment in the course. Ideally, assessment and goal-driven lesson planning are an integrated process that inform and facilitate each other, meaning that assessment for the entire course should be mapped out at the same time as the lesson plans.

Often teachers, as illustrated in the example, have a sudden moment of crisis when they realize they need to think about assessment. At this point, ask yourself the question, "What should my students be able to do now that they couldn't when they entered the course?" This question drives the nature of the actual assessment.

Why Goal-Driven Lesson Planning Matters for Student Progress

Now imagine that it's the very last day of your course. How will you know how much progress your students have made, and how will your students judge their own progress?

To what extent do you base your view of their progress on these factors?

- the number of hours spent per week on English
- the number of exercises filled out in the textbook
- the number of chapters "covered" in the textbook
- the number of new vocabulary words in their notebooks/flash cards
- the number of students who make it through to the end of the semester returning to class

If these are your criteria, there's a problem: students tend not to correctly and spontaneously use, for example, the structures from Chapter 2 when they're in the middle of the exercises for Chapter 4. There's no carryover, no progress, no change. If students can complete the exercises in the textbook on their own, there's no value added by the teacher.

Your view of student progress should be directly tied to your goal-driven lesson planning: How many students can meet how many of the different language goals you have set? Answering that will demonstrate progress in a language class.

With this view of student progress, you can see true change (progress) in students by looking at

- whether students can identify targeted structures/words/pronunciation points (they can say what they worked on throughout the semester)
- whether students can identify strategies to monitor for and self-correct these points
- whether students' speech and/or writing shows fewer errors with targeted structures, as compared to similar speech/writing samples from the beginning of the semester

Using these three criteria as a basis for a final assessment doesn't mean you have to give students individual oral presentations or lengthy final writing assignments in order to assess progress. You can use informal methods to assess student progress, depending on what is right for your particular class.

The End-of-Semester Results of Goal-Driven Lesson Planning

To start to think more about how we as teachers can use goal-driven lesson planning to help students "improve," look at this list of possible student comments on post-course evaluation sheets. Which of these statements would you most want to be said of you and your course? Why?

1. This class was a lot of work, but I think my pronunciation got a lot better.
2. The teacher was really nice, and he was always very understanding. I really felt like this class helped me meet a lot of new friends from different countries.
3. Before this class, I knew I made a lot of mistakes, but now I know what I was doing wrong and how to fix it.
4. I didn't think I really needed this class, but when I look back now at my first essay from this course, I can't believe it's so bad! My writing really improved.
5. The activities in class were a lot of fun. We always played language games, and I liked the topics we read about.

Unless students walk out of your course actually able to say something like what's in numbers 1, 3, or 4, they probably haven't really improved. They may have had an enjoyable experience, but is that really all you want for your students? Think back to your image of the ideal ESL teacher when you answer this question.

Understanding the Reciprocal Nature of Language Goals and Assessment

When you begin the process of lesson planning, you begin by stating what students will be able to do or say if the lesson is successful. Right there, at that very preliminary point, you have drafted the essence of an assessment for that particular lesson. Whether you administer that assessment orally or in writing, formally or informally, in a high-stakes or low-stakes setting, is less important and more dependent on the specifics of your course than the fact that you have it to begin with.

Teachers are sometimes intimidated by the idea of assessment, worried that a bad grade they give a student might be responsible for holding a student back or discouraging him or her. Such teachers equate assessment with grades and might be tempted to seek out programs that do not offer grades in order to avoid what they see as the dilemma of assessment.

But assessing student progress does not mean merely assigning grades. The idea of assessment is simply offering an answer to the question of how you will know your lesson has been successful. Did the lesson work? How will you know? By answering those questions, you are already working on the level of assessment. Even in ungraded courses or in tutoring contexts, you need to know if your lessons are working—and so do students! Students need to have a realistic view of how their language capabilities are changing as a result of the teaching or tutoring.

Teachers who then commit to this view of assessment might find themselves facing what seems like an enormous amount of extra work up front because assessments should be planned before the course begins. The good news here is that if you are using a goal-driven approach to lesson planning, you do not need to do any extra up-front work to plan your assessment: it's already there, built into the lesson plan, as an extra return on your initial investment of time and careful effort.

Reconsidering Different Kinds of Assessments and Their Role in Lesson Planning

Many different kinds of assessments exist. Some are **formal**, such as a graded essay or a quiz, and may be given at the end of a unit or an entire course. Some are **informal**, such as an oral conversation activity that you may be monitoring for accuracy on certain target language points. What is described tends to be examples of **low-stakes** assessments, as opposed to those **high-stakes** exams on which serious outcomes hinge, such as important entrance exams, standardized tests, etc. Graded assessments can then be either **norm-referenced** (in which case students are graded against the norm, the average of others taking that test), **holistic** (in which students are graded on their whole performance, without taking into account individual criteria), or **criterion-referenced** (in which cases students are graded against a set of transparent criteria).

Using criterion-referenced assessment (for student writing, quizzes, oral presentations or other oral activities) removes the subjectivity of holistic grading and the accompanying stress that teachers often feel, while also avoiding the limitations of fitting students into an artificial distribution of grades.

If you use criterion-referenced assessment, you need to be able to specify the criteria in a measurable, observable (i.e., operationalized) way, so that you will be able to clearly state whether students meet the criteria or not. Our description of these criteria as measurable and observable should call to mind the language we used to describe the language goals you set for students. These goals become your criteria for assessment, completing the circle of lesson planning and assessment.

Therefore, with goal-driven lesson planning, for most teachers language goals → criteria for assessment. In some cases, teachers find themselves with an institutional exam that students must take in completing their course. In these cases, your language goals throughout the course should be informed by the exam itself, so that criteria for assessment → language goals.

For teachers who are committed to using the integrated system of goal-driven lesson plans and criterion-referenced assessment, rubrics are tools that will greatly facilitate this process. A rubric is simply a tool for scoring; fill out the rubric ahead of time with your criteria for assessment, and then apply the rubric objectively to all students.

Think of a rubric as a checklist: it's useful for the student when preparing the assignment or studying for the quiz, and it's useful for you, the teacher, when grading the assignment.

For students, rubrics:

- demystify what is required and how it is graded
- clarify what is more and less important
- indicate where individual strengths and weaknesses are

For teachers, rubrics:

- simplify and speed up the process of grading
- give specific information to measure the success of lessons
- make grading less subjective and more defensible

For both teachers and students, rubrics make the process of assessment transparent and clearly related to the goals of individual lessons throughout the course.

Criterion-referenced rubrics use the same language as your operationalized objectives from your lesson plans: The language of instruction becomes the language of assessment.

An Example: A Rubric for Assessing Speaking in a Formal or Informal Context

To assess a student's spontaneous speech, you need a rubric that you can use quickly and easily while the student is actually speaking. However, you also need a rubric that actually informs you of the student's accuracy, so that you don't fall back on subjective holistic judgments. The rubric on page 107 can be used while a student is talking. Use a new row for each utterance (sentence) the student produces; if there are no errors with any of the categories listed, do not make any marks in that row. Use a system of hatch-marks (or checks, cross-marks, etc.) to keep track of errors in the specific categories. Ideally you'd be able to have a recording of the student's speech, so that you could play it back with the student and review it together, but even in the absence of recordings, you can still use the rubric.

The categories on this rubric are appropriate for any intermediate or advanced-level speaking context in which you have addressed the following grammatical points. Alter any of them as necessary for your students. Note that adding more points makes monitoring somewhat difficult during the actual assessment.

Sentence/ Utterance	I. Missing subject	II. Missing verb	III. Missing/ mispron. third singular ending	IV. Missing/ mispron. past regular ending	V. Non-count as count	VI. Missing/ mispron. plural ending	VII. Wrong final intonation
1							
2							
3							
4							
5							
6							
7							
8							
9							
10							
11							
12							
13							
14							

Addressing the Value and Place of Assessment in Ungraded Courses and in Tutoring Situations

Just as goal-driven lesson planning is useful for teachers and tutors in every sort of language-teaching context, so criterion-referenced assessment applies to all language teachers or tutors. Teachers or tutors may sometimes think that because they are working in small classes or one-on-one with students in a program that does not have an end-of-course exam (or grades), the entire idea of assessment is not relevant for them and their students.

Assessment is still necessary because it:

- tells you whether or not your lessons have been working
- gives you a direction for future instruction
- makes clear to students what their progress is

Assessment gives students information necessary for them to move up the ladder of the levels of competence and thereby aids and strengthens the teacher-student partnership. In ungraded situations, a metacognitive assessment is particularly useful because it can show you and the students progress that is happening behind the scenes: it can reveal how students' awareness of a particular error (or aspect of language) has increased, even if their speech still remains unchanged.

Most forms of assessment measure students' performance, the actual language they produce, which is the end result of your lessons. However, before students' performance can change, there are important and requisite changes to their thinking and levels of awareness that must take place. If, at the end of a unit or course, your students can answer these metacognitive questions (orally or in writing), then you will know exactly how much progress they have made:

1. What pronunciation or grammar points did you work on in this unit/course?
2. What strategies help you with these points?
3. What do you know now about these points that you didn't know before?

On the other hand, if all you can say is that students completed the exercises in a given set of chapters or spent a certain number of hours interacting with you in English, then you have no information at all about student progress.

Revisiting Assessment at the Beginning and End of the Course

While students enter your course saying they want to improve their English, what they don't expect or realize is that improving often means changing. The process of language change takes students out of their comfort zones, and to many students, getting it right (i.e., changing their speech to become more target-like) often feels wrong.

As students move up the ladder of levels of competence, they often at first feel like they are moving backward. Although they're not making more mistakes than they were before, they are now aware of their mistakes (Level 2) and realize there is so much they don't know. Metacognitive assessment can help at this point by focusing on students' awareness of their errors, which is itself progress. As students move higher on the ladder, their own awareness of the effort they are expending to correct their errors shows them their progress at Level 3. By Level 4 (automaticity), they need some sort of performance-based assessment to show how their language actually *has* changed because by now they are not conscious of it.

Assessment is therefore the beginning and end of language learning:

- Analyzing learner needs (Chapter 2) is an initial form of assessment.
- Making goal-driven lesson plans (Chapter 3) is also the process of drafting the criteria for your final assessment.
- Offering corrective feedback (Chapter 5) is actually also a form of assessment, as the chart on page 110 shows.

FIGURE 9 ——————————————————————————

Remember our corrective feedback flowchart from Chapter 6?

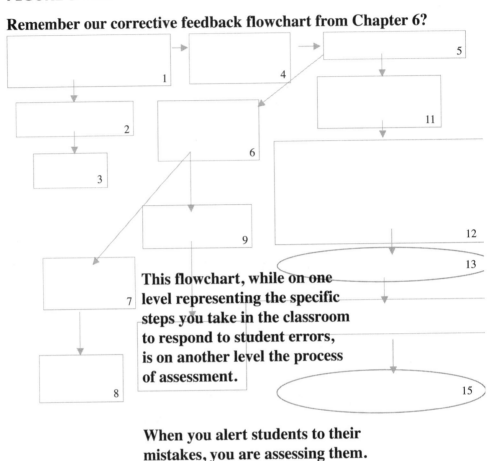

This flowchart, while on one level representing the specific steps you take in the classroom to respond to student errors, is on another level the process of assessment.

When you alert students to their mistakes, you are assessing them.

 REFLECTIVE JOURNAL

One student teacher we worked with was very apprehensive about assessing students. She stated she would only take jobs at language schools without formal grades so that she would never have to give a student a bad grade. What's the problem with this extreme view? How does her avoidance of rubrics and assessment short-change students?

CHAPTER 7

Interaction in the Goal-Driven Classroom

Imagine that you will be mentoring a student teacher next semester in your classroom. You already met once with the student teacher, who came prepared with a list of questions and topics to explore over the course of the observation period. One of the topics is classroom interaction. What does this mean to you? As ESL teachers, we are in the business of enabling students to use the language—which, in the realities of the classroom, means there will be a great deal of language use. How would you describe successful classroom interaction in an ESL context?

This chapter will cover these topics:

- ☑ Moving beyond "Let's just get them talking"
- ☑ Interacting: Teacher to student talk
- ☑ Interacting: Student to teacher talk
- ☑ Interacting: Student to student talk

Moving Beyond "Let's Just Get Them Talking"

Having addressed setting specific language goals and monitoring students' progress toward these goals, we now turn to all the other aspects of managing a classroom. Thinking more about the topics addressed in this chapter will facilitate the success of your goal-driven lessons.

Whatever goals you have, and whatever activities you choose, student speech (output) is going to be key to the success of your lesson. Therefore, let's think about some of the issues that complicate student participation and interaction. When teachers are new to teaching ESL, it is common for them just to want to get students talking and to not think about much beyond that. Working within a goal-driven context, however, we know that there is more to classroom success than "just getting students talking." What some teachers don't think about, however, is how to structure student talk to maximize its effectiveness.

When students are new to learning English, it is very common for them to have a silent period in which they absorb more language than they produce. After that, however, students in a language classroom need to be producing language. It's up to you to structure the class in order to promote and optimize students' verbal output.

Interacting: Teacher to Student Talk

Teachers tend to be very uncomfortable with silence in the classroom. If one or two very communicative students constantly participate, teachers usually are happy to have this participation and may not notice that the majority of students are silent. If an individual classroom does not have any vocal students, then teachers tend to fill the silence with their own talk.

The first step toward encouraging students to talk more in the classroom is for teachers to talk less. When you ask a question, wait longer than you feel comfortable for students to answer. This "wait time" on the part of teachers actually allows for "thought time" on the part of students: students need to process your question, draw up the information for their answer, and then formulate it into words.

HELPFUL HINT

Practice asking a question and waiting quietly at home in front of a mirror. Try a pleasant, neutral expression, and try to relax. Remember that the pause, or brief silence, will be most noticeable—and most uncomfortable—to you. Your students are more likely thinking about the question and not worrying about the pause.

 Eye-Opener

> Most ESL students will tolerate a lot more silence in the classroom than the teacher does. Having silent pauses in the classroom does not mean your lesson is a failure; it means your students have time to think!

The next step toward encouraging students to talk more in the classroom is for teachers to change the way they talk. Ask open-ended questions rather than yes/no questions or single-word response questions.

HELPFUL HINT

Some teachers ask very specific questions, "fishing" for an exact response (also known as the guess-what's-in-my-head type of question). Don't do this! Students are unlikely to phrase their answers in the exact way you had in mind, and likely the exact response is not the point anyway. In your goal-driven lesson plan, script what students will be able to say at the end of the lesson. Remember that the "script" is the lesson's target. You do not need scripted answers to every question you ask throughout the lesson as you guide students toward the target.

> Example of teacher to student interaction while reviewing a grammar-based exercise:
> Yesterday I ____ to school. (walk)

> *T:* Fei, do Number 1.
>
> *S:* walked.
>
> *T:* Read the whole sentence:
>
> *S:* Yesterday I walked to school.

> [typical teacher response:]
>
> *T:* Good! Yes, you need the past tense here, *walked,* even though you have the word *yesterday.* Great!

> [Better teacher response:]
>
> *T:* Okay, tell me about that sentence.
>
> *S:* You need the past tense here, *walked* with *yesterday.*

The typical teacher response in essence says what the student should have internalized about the grammar item in question; you can ask students to say that back to you, thereby producing more language in the classroom and reinforcing the student's internalization of the rule.

HELPFUL HINT

Review the section on Teaching Talk (pages 63–65). This is what students should be saying in the classroom.

Teachers and Talk—
What Happens When Teachers Make Mistakes?

Contrary to what some students may think, teachers do make mistakes. When you make a mistake in the classroom—whether you get a student's name wrong, misspeak, make an error on the board, or mishear a student—acknowledge it. Sometimes a student will point out a mistake, but sometimes you'll realize it yourself (perhaps only a few minutes later). In either case, decide whether the main concern is accuracy of the information given to students (if you misspoke while explaining a grammar point) or sensitivity to students' feelings (if you got a name wrong). Repair as necessary, directing students to check over their class notes if accuracy is the issue.

STUDENT-TEACHER CLARIFICATION QUESTIONS:
WHAT'S THE LANGUAGE OF THE TASK?

Remind students that they can always ask for clarification:
Excuse me, did you mean _____?
Should that be _____?

Interacting: Student to Teacher Talk

REFLECTIVE JOURNALS

Think about these questions. What do you think your practice will be in the classroom for each one, and why?

1. When shy students never volunteer: How do you get students to speak/participate in class?
2. When one student dominates the class: What do you do when one student always speaks up? That person has a right to speak. How do you keep him or her from dominating?
3. When students speak in L1: How do you (think you'll) feel when students speak in L1? Write your response. If your feelings are mixed, make a list: On the one hand/ on the other hand. Did that help?

Teachers tend to struggle with these questions. On one hand, teachers want to be sensitive to students' personalities and cultures; different students may value silence and speech in different ways. On the other hand, however, keeping students in their comfort zones may not advance them toward their language goals: the literature in SLA (Swain, 1985; Pica, Young, & Dougherty, 1987; Gass, 1997) supports the idea that production—student verbal output—is the key to language learning.

Teachers value student participation in the classroom and sometimes judge the success of classes based on the lack of silence. Teachers are sometimes so glad that a student is volunteering something—anything!—that they focus only on the content of what the student says, rather than the accuracy, even of targeted material. It is possible, though, for a teacher to attend both to content and accuracy at the same time. It takes a lot of focused mental energy, but it's possible.

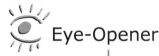 Eye-Opener

> Students' comfort zones: Silence is okay.
> Teachers' comfort zones: Speech—any speech—is preferred.

Students' silence in the classroom may be due to

- quiet/shy/reserved personalities
- cultural prohibitions against displaying knowledge
- different schema for classroom behavior

  These students think they're learning and being good students; they're not necessarily unhappy with the silence. In fact, they may be unhappy with students who *do* speak up in class and may feel that those students are taking time away from the teacher.

- confusion about the question asked.

  These students need to be formulating a clarification request in order to move forward. If students then don't have the language to ask for clarification and/or don't know that it's appropriate to ask, then the classroom interaction abruptly stops, and teachers may not know why.

STUDENT-TEACHER CLARIFICATION QUESTIONS:
WHAT'S THE LANGUAGE OF THE TASK?

Add this classroom language to your lesson plans as goals for students! Are your students able to ask these questions, and do they understand that it's appropriate to do so?

What does ____ mean? (instead of "What's mean _____?")

How do you say _____? (instead of "How to say _____?")

What's the question again?

What page are we on?

Could you repeat that?

Interacting: Student to Student Talk

Some students have different schema for what a classroom is and what kinds of talk are appropriate in the classroom. You may find students who think that the preferred mode of communication is only between themselves and the teacher. You need to foster student to student interaction for two primary reasons: first, there are clear benefits to students' language abilities as a result of such interaction (Long, 1980); second, students will need to be able to communicate effectively with their peers in other classroom-type situations (community college, college or university, job training, etc.). Figure 10 shows two kinds of classroom interaction. In general, more student-to-student interaction is preferable.

Depending on the size of your classroom, put students in pairs or small groups to foster interaction. You might choose to group students based on proximity in the classroom, student preference, ability levels, language backgrounds, personality types, or culture or nationality. There is no right grouping scheme for any particular class; the chart on page 118 considers some advantages and disadvantages of each.

FIGURE 10
Two Kinds of Classroom Interaction

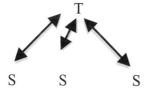 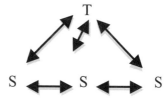

HELPFUL HINT

Students do not need to know your rationale for the grouping. Mix the groups up every class, for example, so that students are used to this process. Do not just let students work with their friends or their seatmates every time simply because that is the simplest logistically; students need interaction with other classmates and practice in following directions and group protocols.

If you decide to group students based on any of the factors in the chart (other than random or proximity), you will likely have a list of groups written before the class session begins. When starting the group activity, give your instructions to the class in the most natural way possible. For example, when reading off a list of paired names, most native speakers would read the names with small pauses between individual names and larger pauses between pairs (or sets). Forcing students to attend to the information conveyed in your pauses (i.e., thought groups) is a great help to students' listening comprehension abilities and prepares them for contexts beyond your classroom.

Grouping Type	Advantages	Disadvantages
Classroom proximity	logistically easy	groups tend to be the same throughout the semester, as students tend to sit in the same areas; other factors not taken into account
Student preference	pleasing to students	groups may tend to be the same throughout the semester; groups may not challenge or stretch students; other factors not taken into account
Same ability level	allows targeted feedback to different groups; allows more able groups to move on and complete more/different activities while lower-level groups solidify target material	use selectively so as not to stigmatize lower-ability groups
Mixed ability level	allows stronger students to assist weaker ones to together work on target material	sometimes the strong students may dominate and the weaker ones do not actually participate; alternatively, sometimes the strong students may disengage from the activity
Same language background	allows students to use shared L1 and background knowledge to work on target material	allows students to use shared L1 and background knowledge to work on target material
Mixed personality type	allows able but shy students to speak up in a less intimidating environment	might allow vocal students to dominate
Same personality type	forces vocal students to encounter other vocal students in a small group and negotiate together; allows shyer students to speak up without vocal students dominating	silent group may engage with task but may never actually interact with each other
Mixed culture or nationality	students get to interact with classmates from other cultures	students from conflicting countries and/or vastly different cultures may, until they get to know each other, be so uncomfortable that they disengage
Random/counting off	students work with classmates they don't normally work or sit with; students get practice with this common kind of grouping technique	groups are essentially random, without taking any other factors into account

STUDENT-STUDENT GROUP INTERACTION: ─────── WHAT'S THE LANGUAGE OF THE TASK?

Tell your students to introduce themselves to each other when working in a new group! Remind them that they can always ask their groupmates to stay focused on the assigned task.

"Hi, I'm _____."

"Sorry, what did you say your name was?"

"How do you spell your name?"

"So, what are we supposed to be doing?"

SPOTLIGHT ON RESEARCH ─────────────────

What does SLA theory have to say about conversation, student output, and classroom interaction?

In the 1970s and 1980s, Stephen Krashen (1985) proposed the comprehensible input hypothesis, arguing that comprehensible input—language provided to students from any source—is necessary and sufficient for SLA to occur.

In the 1980s, the field of SLA then moved to the next level with the comprehensible output hypothesis. This claims that input alone is insufficient: learners must be pushed to produce language (forced or pushed output). SLA then occurs as a result of learners noticing the gap between their imperfect output and listeners' attempts to clarify/restate (Swain, 1985).

Beginning in 1980, Michael Long (1980) proposed the interaction hypothesis, which claims that pushed output best occurs during student to student interactions, making such interactions key for SLA to occur.

Eye-Opener

Fact: ESL teachers tend to be more accommodating of students' errors than the world at large.

Conclusion: We are doing our students a disservice if we do not equip them for less accommodating conversational partners.

Consequences: We need to teach students how to troubleshoot communication breakdowns from both the point of view of speaker and listener.

Use the graphic on page 120 with students to help them negotiate for meaning.

LANGUAGE STRATEGY:
AVOIDING COMMUNICATION BREAKDOWNS

Remember that successful communication works on two levels: You can under-stand others, and others can understand you. When others don't understand you, communication begins to break down. You can be more active in avoiding communication breakdowns: If you pay attention to these signs, you'll be able to check for and repair a breakdown in communication.

Look for: puzzled stares, tilted heads, frowns

Listen for: requests for repetition, requests for clarification, answers that don't make sense

Some students feel that they don't need to make changes to their English because they're getting along all right: other people understand them. But, what may be happening is that the students' listeners are doing all the work!

Communication should be balanced. Don't make your listeners do all the work of trying to understand you: you also need to work on being understood.

STUDENT-STUDENT CLARIFICATION QUESTIONS:——
WHAT'S THE LANGUAGE OF THE TASK?

Make sure your students can say these all-purpose clarification requests. Students need to know that, when working in a group, it's appropriate and even required to ask peers for clarification when they do not understand.

I'm sorry, I don't understand.

Did you mean _____?

More specific requests can be formed by asking targeted questions (often with contrastive stress, for example: *Who's* coming to visit you Saturday?) or by repeating part of the utterance and pointing to the source of the problem (again often with contrastive stress, for example: You're taking classes *where*?)

REFLECTIVE JOURNAL

Given everything discussed in this chapter (including grouping strategies, explicit teaching of classroom language, difference schemas for classroom behavior, etc.), how would you handle this situation?

CASE STUDY: SILENT STUDENTS ——

Early in the semester, an ESL teacher who has adopted the goal-driven classroom strategy is frustrated with the way a specific activity worked in class. He diagnosed student needs, set specific language goals, introduced the target structure, selected an appropriate activity to advance students toward the goal, explained the activity, and divided the students into groups to do the activity. Students remained almost completely silent in their groups and did not really interact with each other. When he walked around the room to monitor students, he noticed that individual students were completing the handout on their own and that students were not working together.

What could account for this situation?

What is your plan to address classroom interaction more explicitly in your own teaching as a result of this chapter?

CHAPTER 8

Managing the Goal-Driven Classroom

Think about it

Imagine that you're about to walk into the classroom on the first day of a new semester. You've prepared for the class extensively, including using some of the materials in this book to craft an initial diagnostic plan and tentative goal-driven lesson plans and lesson sequences. As veteran teachers have come to learn, there are inevitably things that intervene in the execution of even the best-laid classroom plans. What might you anticipate as typical beginning-of-the-semester distractions, and how will you cope with these? What kinds of organizational strategies do/will you use to keep track of the moment-to-moment realities of the classroom?

This chapter will cover these topics:

- ☑ Choosing appropriate activities and materials
- ☑ Maximizing blackboard use
- ☑ Using teacher tools for classroom management
- ☑ Real-time decision-making for teacher and tutors

Choosing Appropriate Activities and Materials

As the example illustrates, there is more to successful execution of a lesson plan than just having a plan to begin with. This chapter helps you organize some of the sometimes overlooked aspects of teaching and classroom management, starting with the specific choice of activities and moving on to other practical matters. In all cases, thinking about these things in advance will help you effectively execute your goal-driven lesson plan.

Before entering the classroom, you'll need to think about the choice of activities and materials for the lesson. In other words, you need to create a lesson sequence for your class to complement your goal-driven lesson plan. Beyond the typical textbook exercises and activities (fill-in-the-blanks, matching columns, simple interview questions, etc.), there are many more interactive activities that teachers turn to time and again in the classroom. Eight types of activities are described that will get students talking because in all language classrooms, after all, language production (i.e., speech) is essential. We give specific examples of a few of the less well-known activity types, and some points to consider when choosing an activity to slot into your lesson plan are suggested.

Chain Story

Example:
Directions: Step 1: Co-create a word bank of regular verbs (do not add –*ed*) based on course content.

walk	play	call	visit	ask	help	decide	practice
fix	wait	finish	move	want	arrange	copy	include

Step 2: Ask students to assign each verb to one of three columns according to the ending: [t] [d] [Id].

t	d	Id
walk	play	visit

Step 3: Practice the pronunciation for each verb, column by column.

Step 4: Expand the verbs. For each verb, add words/ phrases.

t	d	Id
walked a mile	played a game	visited a friend
finished my homework	arranged a meeting	waited for the bus

Step 5: Student 1 selects a verb phrase and uses the frame: *Yesterday I…(walked a mile).* Student 2 selects a different phrase, repeats Student 1's contribution, and adds his or her own: *Yesterday, X walked a mile and I … (called a friend).* Student 3 selects, repeats 1 and 2, adds his or her own.

**WHEN WOULD I WANT TO USE THIS TYPE OF ACTIVITY
IN THE CLASSROOM? WHAT BENEFITS DOES IT OFFER?**

Because a chain story requires a great deal of repetition, you may want to use it when students need more practice to master a new pattern, structure, pronunciation, or vocabulary set. This type of activity involves both speaking and listening because it forces students to pay attention to what other students have already said.

Strip Story

Example:
Strip Story for Past Tense and Participle Regular Verbs:
The Isabella Stewart Gardner Museum Theft
    For this activity, one group of 13 volunteers follows these steps.

1: Look at the sentences. Each person in your group is responsible for one sentence. Copy your sentence onto an index card. Mark your sentence for linking and the sounds of the past tense endings.

2: Close your book and memorize your sentence. Give your index card to your teacher (or group leader).

3: As a group, say your sentences aloud and try to put them in order to tell the story. Remember linking and the sounds of the -*ed* ending when you say your sentence aloud. When you think the sentences are in order, recite your sentences in order.

Directions for the rest of class:

For small classes: Get together around a desk and spread out the index cards from the group of volunteers. As a group, put the cards in order to tell a story. When everyone is finished, check the order of the students' sentences.

For large classes: Work with a partner to put the sentences below in order. Make sure to read them aloud for linking and *-ed* endings.

For all classes: Listen to the members of the small group. Are they saying the *-ed* endings correctly? For example, make sure *solved* has only one syllable.

A. ____ In 1903, she turned her home into a museum and opened it to the public.

B. ____ Almost 20 years have passed, and the FBI admitted it still has not identified the thieves or located the masterpieces.

C. ____ In 1891, a Boston woman named Isabella Stuart Gardner inherited a fortune.

D. ____ The reporter thinks he solved the case.

E. ____ The stolen art included three Rembrandts and a painting by Vermeer called *The Concert*.

F. ____ On March 18, 1990, the Gardner Museum was robbed by two unknown men.

G. ____ In 2009, a journalist published a book about the robbery.

H. ____ Before she passed away in 1924, Gardner willed her home to the City of Boston.

I. ____ That night, the thieves escaped with thirteen works of art.

J. ____ The next day, the estimated value was reported to be over $300 million.

K. ____ The FBI investigated the case; they called it the biggest art theft in U.S. history.

L. ____ She traveled the world in the 1890s and collected works of art.

M. ____ They were dressed as police officers.

When would I want to use this type of activity in the classroom? What benefits does it offer?

A strip story is an interactive sequencing task that involves less repetition than a chain story but more attention to meaning. It can provide students with more practice using a given structure, but it also forces students to talk about their sequencing decisions and therefore encourages a great deal of student-student interaction.

Human Scavenger Hunt (Find Someone Who)

Example:
Find someone who. . .

> has at least two sisters
> has more brothers than sisters
> has four living grandparents
> has a younger brother

When would I want to use this type of activity in the classroom?
What benefits does it offer?

By asking many questions of their classmates, students have to move and that produces a good amount of energy in the classroom. Even more important, though, the activity requires students to manipulate sentences and questions, working with question word-order and the English auxiliary system. There are real-world language benefits to this type of activity.

Interactive Matching Columns

Example:
Matching: In your neighborhood

There are four two-person dialogues for this activity.
Work in groups of eight students or count off from 1 to 5 around the room.
Number the students in your group from 1 to 5 and copy the corresponding sentence on a separate piece of paper.
For example, Student 1 copies Sentence 1, and so on.

Memorize your sentence, and be ready to say it aloud to your group.
Your goal is to find a student whose sentence completes your dialogue, like

I need to get some gas.	There's a post office down the street.
I need to get some milk.	There's a bus stop two blocks away.
I need to mail a package.	There's a pay phone across the street.
I need to make a phone call.	There's a gas station on the corner.
I need to catch a bus.	There's a grocery store down the block.

When would I want to use this type of activity in the classroom?
What benefits does it offer?

This type of activity gets students moving around the classroom and interacting with each other, while paying attention to meaning. You can use this type of activity to focus on any aspect of the language. In the example, students are explicitly focused on the use of existential *there* in English; they also can pay attention to linking and thought groups for clearer connected speech (*There's a* → *Thereza*). Furthermore, the sample exercise shows students real-world examples of when to use a workbook structure (*there is/there are*).

Conflict-Resolution Activity

Example:
Contrastive Stress Exercise: Mini-Conflict Resolution Activity

> *Classroom set up for large or small classes*
> There are four two-person dialogues for the following activity.
> Work in groups of eight students or count off from 1 to 8 around the room.
> Number the students in your group from 1 to 8 and copy the corresponding sentence on a separate piece of paper.
> For example, Student 1 copies Sentence 1, and so on.
>
> Mark your sentence for linking, deletion, reduction, and alteration.
> Mark your sentence for standard sentence stress OR contrastive stress if appropriate.
> Memorize your sentence and be ready to say it aloud to your group.
> Your goal is to find a student whose sentence completes your dialogue.

Rules: Remember—each side is OUT TO WIN

1. Here are the pants that you brought in. That'll be $4.
2. I'm not looking for men's coats; I'm looking for women's coats.
3. I didn't stay in room #12; I stayed in room #11.
4. I didn't bring in pants; I brought in shirts.
5. The flight to Dulles International Airport leaves from Gate 32B.
6. Room #12 made some long-distance calls. That'll be $72.
7. Men's coats are on the third floor.
8. I'm not going to Dulles, I'm going to Dallas.

Source: *Sound Concepts* by M. Reed and C. Michaud, 2005, McGraw-Hill. Used with permission.

When would I want to use this type of activity in the classroom?
What benefits does it offer?

This type of activity picks up where the previous type leaves off. In addition to requiring students to move around, interact with each other, and focus on the meaning of their sentences, there is an element of role-playing and extended conversation in this activity. As written, the example focuses students on contrastive stress (<u>I'm not going to Dulles, I'm going to *Dallas*</u>), without which any conversation based on this activity would be meaningless. Students can perform their role-plays for the class, and the class could even offer feedback on their accuracy and/or pronunciation.

Information-Gap Activity

When would I want to use this type of activity in the classroom?
What benefits does it offer?

You will certainly see examples of this type of activity in textbooks; in many cases, these activities consist of intricately designed—but somewhat artificial— schedules and charts for a pair of students to work from. The benefits of this type of activity are getting students talking, asking and answering questions that they genuinely don't know the answers to, while using particular constructions that you've targeted.

Role-Play

When would I want to use this type of activity in the classroom?
What benefits does it offer?

Role-plays are by nature open-ended, but depending on how you set them up, you can focus students fairly narrowly (as in our example). The benefit, of course, is practice in real-world interaction; role-plays are particularly suited to working on the pragmatics of English—speech-acts such as greetings, leave-takings, and everything in between.

Debate

When would I want to use this type of activity in the classroom?
What benefits does it offer?

Almost every conversational ESL class includes at least one debate; students are used to being asked to debate topics ranging from the light-hearted to the serious. Well-set-up debates require students to work together in a group, interacting with each other and negotiating for meaning without a teacher stepping in to solve language dilemmas. Debates can allow students to practice a particular set of vocabulary as well as the language of logical argumentation in an open-ended way.

For these and other types of activities—indeed, for everything you do in the classroom, from "going over the homework" on up—you must be sure you have a rationale for including them. In other words, how will each activity advance students toward the particular goals of the lesson?

Assuming that you've already written your goal-driven lesson plan, draft a single-page, see-at-a-glance lesson sequence to bring into the classroom with you. Such a document may contain a quick list of activities down the left-hand side of the page with a note at right next to each activity, reminding you of which objective(s) it will help students meet. Alternatively, you might organize your page as shown here, with the goals on the left-hand side of the page and activities needed to reach these goals on the right.

Goal	*Activity*
Students will practice using existential *there* in supplied contexts.	Interactive matching columns with *need to/there's a*
Students will link consonant to vowel sounds from word to word appropriately.	
Students will supply and use existential *there* in new contexts when appropriate.	Extension activity with student-supplied content

Maximizing Blackboard Use

Most teachers use the blackboard (or whiteboard, or greenboard, etc.) routinely in their classroom; in fact, many teachers will even say they find it hard to teach without one! But most teachers don't think in advance about what precisely they will put on the board, much less what their board will look like at the end of a specific lesson.

Because whatever you write on the board, students will copy; it's important to

- Think about what, and think about where.
- Know why everything that's on the board is there.
- Not let errors stay on the board.

Some common problems with the way teachers use the board in their classrooms are given:

1. Some teachers write everything on the board, from directions for activities to homework assignments including sentences from the homework that students are reviewing in class.

   Problem: This approach, at a very basic level, wastes the time it takes teachers to write on the board without necessarily adding any value to the lesson. It also risks making students overly reliant on the board for information that in "real" (i.e., non-ESL) classrooms, teachers tend to deliver orally rather than in writing.

2. Sometimes teachers ask students to put up on the board their sentences or paragraphs from a specific activity for everyone to look at together.

   Problem: This approach takes up a great deal of classroom time for an arguable payoff, with a small subset of the class finding chalk, finding space, and writing on the board while the majority of the class stares at their backs. In addition, student sentences almost always contain errors, and teachers are faced with the dilemma of leaving the errors on the board (for other students to copy down) or else correcting every single error, even those that are beyond the focus of the lesson at hand.

3. Other teachers put things up on the board at random throughout the lesson, resulting in an incoherent jumble.

   Problem: Teachers who don't have a clear plan for their blackboard risk detracting from their focus by obscuring the underlying logic and organization of the lesson. As a result, students may mistakenly focus on tangential points, or may conflate two different aspects of the lesson into one.

In each of these cases, the solution is for teachers to plan their blackboard use ahead of time, when they plan their lessons. Just as you think about what directions you're going to give students for different activities or how long activities will take, you should think about what your blackboard will look like, when you'll be writing on it, and why.

Ask yourself these questions when planning your lesson:

1. What will the board look like at every step of the lesson?
2. Why am I writing these things on the board? What does seeing them visually add to the lesson?
3. When will I write things on the board?
4. What will students be doing while I write on the board?
5. What will the board look like at the end of the lesson?
6. Where are the different components of the lesson in relation to each other—should the material be written in columns, sections, etc.?

One practical tip is to make a note on your copy of your lesson plan, handout, or textbook about what you will put on the board and when. Some teachers use a different colored pen to remind themselves that they're going to put this information up on the board; others use an abbreviation (such as "BB") for what goes on the blackboard next to the relevant part of their notes.

Ultimately, you have to make clear to yourself what you are writing on the board, as well as where, when, and why. If it's not clear to you, it certainly won't be clear to students.

HELPFUL HINT

If your lesson targets punctuation points—for example, run-on sentences—you will need to exaggerate your punctuation on the board to be sure students see and attend to it.

An example of an orderly blackboard for a lesson on the pronunciation of plural count nouns is shown in Figure 11. If you asked students before the lesson to come in with the names of three countable items they use in their fields of academic study, you know that your students can supply the content (vocabulary) for the day. Put these words up on the board, sorting them into categories with help from the students as they pick up on your organizing principle. Later, add the reminder at bottom right about unvoiced and sibilant sounds, label the top of the columns with the sound of the plural ending, and add the rule at the top right about how to pronounce the endings.

FIGURE 11 ———————————————————————————————
Planning Your Blackboard

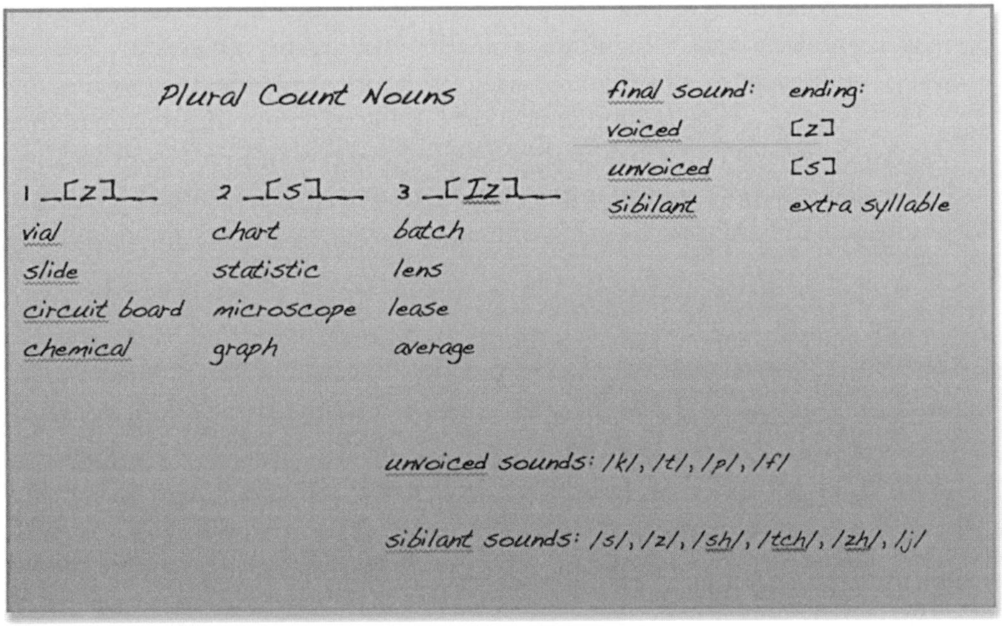

Plural Count Nouns

final sound:	ending:
voiced	[z]
unvoiced	[s]
sibilant	extra syllable

1 _[z]_   2 _[s]_   3 _[Iz]_

vial   chart   batch
slide   statistic   lens
circuit board   microscope   lease
chemical   graph   average

unvoiced sounds: /k/, /t/, /p/, /f/

sibilant sounds: /s/, /z/, /sh/, /tch/, /zh/, /j/

Using Teacher Tools for Classroom Management

Different institutions have different requirements for the paperwork that accompanies teaching; you may be asked to fill out school-specific attendance sheets, lesson plans, classroom logs, etc. Beyond any institutional and/or government requirements, however, you will find it useful to have some sort of system for yourself to keep track of these types of things for your classes:

- Attendance and lateness
- Homework, quiz, etc., scores/grades
- Goal-driven lesson plans (cumulatively—lessons, units, semester, etc.)
- Actual classroom activities
- Follow-up notes to yourself
- Student errors that you are currently monitoring for
- Student errors that you may address and/or monitor for in the future

Any sort of organizational system is fine, but you need a system. Sometimes teachers find it useful to keep a separate notebook for each course, or separate sections in a single notebook. Others prefer to use folders, which may then also contain handouts you give out on any given day. Regardless of your system (which you will probably fine-tune during your first few courses and/or semesters), you need to be able to access this information at will. Keeping track of what specific student errors you're monitoring for in a given class is particularly important if you're teaching multiple levels. For example, in an intermediate integrated-skills class you may be monitoring for:

- third-person singular present tense endings
- count noun plurals for things in general
- past participles in perfect tenses and passive voice
- correct question word order (auxiliaries, etc.)

REFLECTIVE JOURNAL—CLASSROOM MANAGEMENT ISSUES

1. When students arrive late:

   What are the possible responses? List three. What will your late policy be? How will you notify students of it?

2. Learning students' names:

   How do you learn people's names? Do you have to see the name in writing?

   How do you plan to learn your students' names? Write down your intended strategy.

3. When students "cheat" on tests or exams:

   Why is the word in quotes? Has it ever happened in you class? How was/should it be handled?

Real-Time Decision-Making for Teacher and Tutors

Everything addressed up to this point is important to consider before setting foot in the classroom. Finally we examine those few things that you must consider when they occur in the classroom in the middle of a lesson: the unpredictable questions from students.

What happens when a student asks a question in the classroom? Sometimes teachers don't know what to do with student questions. Figure 12 walks you through a decision-making process you can use, quickly, whenever a student asks a question.

FIGURE 12

When a Student Asks a Question: Deciding How to Respond

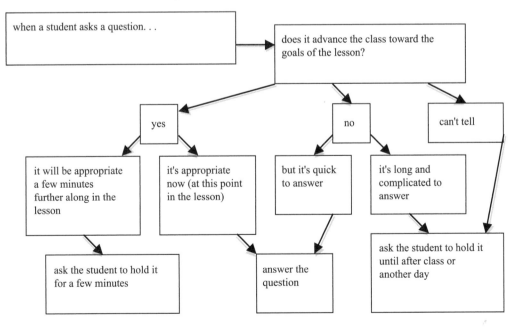

Many teachers may feel that the tables, comparisons, flowcharts, and suggestions in these last two chapters (Chapters 7–8) are the most practical, hands-on help for teaching. We hope that these tools are useful for you in your teaching, and while they can certainly be helpful to you, they are not key to student success. The key to student success is setting and monitoring progress toward specific, measurable, observable language goals. The tools in the last two chapters can facilitate the process of getting students to achieve specific language goals.

REFLECTIVE JOURNAL

How have your feelings on lesson plans and language goals changed as a result of reading this book?

What will you do differently in your teaching, and why?

What two or three specific things (concepts, flowcharts, strategies, etc.) are for you the take-away message of this book that will help revitalize your teaching?

A Final Note ————————————————————————

We hope this book has been helpful to you. We wrote it, in part, because all too often practicing ESL teachers don't have a community of colleagues to talk about these issues with on a regular basis. If you used this book as part of a Master's-level teaching practicum or methods course, then you are lucky to have a built-in community, but if you read through this book on your own, then we think the reflective questions and journals are all the more important in helping you make sense of our ideas and of your personal approach to teaching. Please feel free to contact us to let us know how goal-driven lesson planning is working for you in your classrooms!

—Marnie and Christina

References ───────────────────────────────────────

Allwright, R. (1975). Problems in the study of the language teacher's treatment of learner error. In M. K. Burt & H. C. Dulay (Eds.), *On TESOL '75: New directions in second language learning, teaching, and bilingual education* (pp. 96–109). Washington, DC: TESOL.

Andrews, K. L. Z. (2007). The effects of implicit and explicit instruction on simple and complex grammatical structures for adult English language learners. *TESL. Ed. 11*(2), 1–15.

Armington, S. (1993/94). Teaching pronunciation at the micro-level: Using keywords from student speech. *TESOL Journal, 2*(3), 27.

Beebe, L. (1978). Teaching pronunciation: Why we should be. *Idiom, 9*(2).

Block, D. (1992). Metaphors we teach and live by. *Prospect, 7*(3), 42–55.

Corder, S. P. (1967). The significance of learners' errors. *International Review of Applied Linguistics, 5*, 161–170.

Derwing, T., & M. Rossiter. (2002). ESL learners' perceptions of their pronunciation needs and strategies. *System 30*(2), 155–166.

Ellis, R., Basturkmen, H., & S. Loewen. (2001). Learner uptake in communicative ESL lessons. *Language Learning, 51*(2), 281–318.

Gass, S. (1997). *Input, interaction, and the second language learner*. Mahwah, NJ: Lawrence Erlbaum.

Guerrero, M. C. M. de, and Villamil, O. S. (2000). Exploring teachers' roles through metaphor analysis. *TESOL Quarterly 34*, 341–351.

Hendrickson, J. M. (1978). Error correction in foreign language teaching: Recent theory, research, and practice. *Modern Language Journal, 62*, 388–392.

Hermann, G. (1980). "Attitudes and success in children's learning of English as a Second Language: The motivational vs. resultative hypothesis." *English Language Teaching Journal, 34*, 247–254.

International Phonetic Association (1999) *Handbook of the international phonetic association.* Cambridge, UK: Cambridge University Press.

Krashen, S. (1985). *The input hypothesis: Issues and implications.* New York: Longman.

Lightburn, P., & Spade, N. (1990). Focus on form and second language learning. *Studies in Second Language Acquisition, 6*, 186–214.

Loewen, S. (2005). Incidental focus on form and second language acquisition. *Studies in Second Language Acquisition, 27*, 361–386.

Long, M. H. (1980). *Input, interaction and second language acquisition*. Unpublished doctoral dissertation, University of California, Los Angeles.

———. (1991). Focus on form: A design feature in language teaching methodology. In K. de Bot, D. Coste, R. Ginsheng, & C. Kuensch (Eds.), *Foreign language research in cross-cultural perspective.* Amsterdam: John Benjamins.

Major, R. C. (1988). Interlanguage phonetics and phonology: An introduction. *Studies in Second Language Acquisition, 20,* 131–137.

Major, R. (1995). Native and nonnative phonological representations. *International Review of Applied Linguistics, 33*(2), 109–127.

Panova, I., & Lyster, R. (2002). Patterns of corrective feedback and uptake in an adult ESL classroom. *TESOL Quarterly, 36*(4), 573–595.

Pica, T., Young, R., & Dougherty, C. (1987). The impacts of interaction on comprehension. *TESOL Quarterly, 21*(4), 737–758.

Reed, M., & Michaud, C. (2005). *Sound concepts: An integrated pronunciation course.* New York: McGraw-Hill.

Strong, M. H. (1984). "Integrative motivation: Cause or result of successful second language acquisition?" *Language Learning, 34*(3), 1–14.

Swain, M. (1985). Communicative competence: Some roles of comprehensible input and comprehensible output in its development. In S. Gass & C. Madden (Eds.), *Input in second language acquisition* (pp. 235–256). New York: Newbury House.

Swann, M., & Smith, B. (2001). *Learner English: A teacher's guide to interference and other problems* (2nd ed.). Cambridge, UK: Cambridge University Press.

Varonis, E., & Gass, S. (1982). "The Comprehensibility of Non-Native Speakers." *Language Acquisition, 5,* 235–256.

Wiggins, G., & McTighe, J. (2005). *Understanding by design* (Expanded 2nd ed.). Alexandria, VA: Association for Supervision and Curriculum Development.